WHO IS THIS GOD?

by Ray Pippin

All scriptures quotations are taken from the New King James Version unless otherwise noted. "New King James. Copyright © 1982, by Thomas Nelson, Inc. Used by permission. All rights reserved."

Some quotations noted NIV are from "The Holy Bible, New International Version ®, NIV ® copyright © 1973,1978,1984,2011 by Biblica, Inc. Used by permission worldwide.

Some quotations noted ASV are from American Standard Version Renewed 1929. All rights reserved. Used by permission.

New English Bible (NEB) copyright © 1961, 1970 by the delegates of the Oxford University press and the Syndics of the Cambridge University Press. Used by permission.

Scripture quotations marked (NLT) are taken from the Holy Bible, New Living Translation, copyright © 1996, 2004, 2007 by Tyndale House Foundation. Used by permission of Tyndale House Publishers, Inc., Carol Stream , Illinois 60188 . All rights reserved.

Words from songs or poems used are public domain. With acknowledgement noted.

Acknowledgements

Special thanks to my wife, Nora, who endured hours of silence as I pondered over the right words to say. She also had the courage to tell me when another word would say it better.

I can remember preachers who stayed in our home when I was growing up who encouraged me to become a preacher. Later when I was preaching, some people would say they had never heard the nature of God talked about. I remember asking an audience of approximately two hundred how many had ever heard one full sermon on the character of God. Only two or three held up their hands. Then, from time to time others would say I should write some of these things down. Also shortly after we were married, my wife began to encourage me to do this too.

My nine grandchildren; twenty (and still counting) great-grandchildren as well as my three daughters, Joy, Jo and Paula (who seem to think I am an above average dad) all keep me going when the going gets tough.

My daughter, Joy, and her husband, Darrel Emerson, have spent hours looking over and correcting my mistakes while offering some good advice. Without their help, this book could not have published.

A special thanks to Stephen Hayes for doing a great job on the illustration for the cover.

To each my heartfelt thanks. To the One and Only true God, who has blessed me more than I could have ever dreamed and is the subject of this volume, be all glory both now and forever more. Ray

Dedication

Ardel and Isabell Dill Pippin

This book is dedicated to the memory of my parents, Ardel and Isabell Dill Pippin. They were born in Jackson County, Tennessee. They spent the early years of their marriage in California. The remainder of their life was spent in Tennessee.

Not a day goes by that I don't think of them. I grew up believing I had the greatest man to walk the earth for a father and a mother who stood by his side all the way. The succeeding years have not changed my mind. My father did most of the preaching, song leading and teaching Bible classes in the little church at Union Hill. I only pray that at least some of what rubbed off on me will rub off on my children, grandchildren and great-grandchildren who at this time total 31 and growing. Some things are not inherited from our parents, but they are taught. My dream is for them to love God with all their being and their neighbor as themselves.

This book is written especially for them.

Ray

Table of Contents

Foreword

How can we who are finite come to know the One who is infinite? How can man who is so limited understand the One who has no limits? How can we understand that which is beyond our comprehension? How can we touch that which is untouchable? How do we deal with One who is not only so high above us, but His ways and thoughts are as high above us as the heavens are above the earth?

Ray, in a simple, yet, challenging and thought provoking way, leads us in a journey that allows this One to reveal Himself to us in His own way. He gives us everything we need that we may know Him, and trusting Him, we will give Him the devotion He is worthy to receive. It really is a book about God. When you have finished with this little volume, you may never read your Bible the same way.

Chapter One

GETTING TO KNOW GOD

"And Pharaoh said, 'Who is the LORD, that I should obey His voice to let Israel go? I do not know the LORD, nor will I let Israel go.'" (Ex 5:2)

"That I may know Him and the power of His resurrection, and the fellowship of His sufferings, being conformed to His death, if, by any means, I may attain to the resurrection from the dead." (Phil 3:10-11)

1

When God's people were slaves in Egypt under the Pharaoh of that time, none of us would classify him as a good king. In fact, most would agree he was wicked. Some might go so far as to say he was stupid. Of all the terrible things he did, and certainly the many bad decisions he made, there is one good question he asked.

When God sent Moses and Aaron to Pharaoh and told him to *"let my people go"*. Pharaoh asked one good question when he said,

"Who is the Lord that I should obey his voice and let Israel go? (Ex 5:2a)

Really, it was a good question. No one should just blindly obey the orders of anyone that comes along claiming to be God. Up to this time, Pharaoh probably had not been interested one way or the other concerning the God of these slaves. He probably thought if their god was very much of a god they would not be slaves. Furthermore, I have plenty of my own gods to listen to; I don't need to be bothered with another.

Because God had told Moses before how Pharaoh would react and what He in turn would do to convince him, I can imagine Moses saying to himself, just wait and see what this God is about to do. When God is finished with the ten plagues, there will be no doubt in your mind just who He is. And sure enough when God was finished with the tenth plague, there was no doubt in Pharaoh's mind. This God is different. He could see the gods of Egypt were no match for this God. In the end, Pharaoh was not only willing to let the people go, he ordered them to leave. We don't really know how long Pharaoh lived after that encounter. We do know he hardened his heart again and continued to make bad choices but one thing for sure, there had been a moment in time when Pharaoh had to face the fact this God is different. His magicians, who he considered representatives of his gods, knew better than to attempt to duplicate this one. This God controls life and that makes all the difference.

3

What you and I believe about this God likewise will determine how we react to what He says to us as well. Someone has said, and it's so true, the most important thing about any individual is not what he or she will do under a given set of circumstances but what deep in their heart they believe their God to be like. What we believe about God is not just academic but it will guide the way we live our lives and as a result will determine our eternal destiny.

Jesus told the story of three men who were given talents (responsibility) by their master. One received five talents, another received two and another was given only one. The one talent man failed to use his talent but took it and buried it. When his master returned and called him to account he offered this excuse.

"I knew you are a hard man, harvesting where you have not sown and gathering where you had not scattered seed. So I was afraid and went and hid your talent in the ground. See, here is what belongs to you."(Matt 25:24-25)

4

His master took the talent from him called him a wicked individual and cast him into outer darkness. (Matt 25:14-30). We have heard all kinds of excuses for this one talent man's actions. In the end, his problem was very basic, he had the wrong idea of his master; he thought he was different than he really was. Failure to understand the true nature of God is the root cause of most of the problems, not only in the world in general, but in the church as well. Any teaching of false doctrine as well as any failure in making application of moral law to society can be traced to some degree to a misunderstanding or false belief about who this God really is.

We all have the desire to know as much about one another as we can. This is good. We need to understand each other to live together in peace and a more productive way. It does seem odd that many seem to be content to know very little about who this God really is; at least they seem content with what they have imagined Him to be.

The Hebrew writer seemed to think it was important when he wrote:

*"And without faith, it is impossible to
please God, for anyone who comes
to Him must believe that He exists
and that He rewards those who
earnestly seek Him.
(Heb 11:6) NIV*

When we say we believe God exists, we
are making a fundamental statement that is
the very basis of our faith. This is really
where it begins. A lot has been written on
the outside evidence that supports our faith.
This is all well and good. However, the
greatest proof of the existence of God is
God himself. He needs no other support.
When the Bible writer began in Genesis one
he just simply said, *"In the beginning
God..."* He offers no further proof as if none
was needed. I often wonder how these
inspired men would have responded had
someone asked for some additional proof.
Would they have laughed?

It is no wonder Paul would declare in
Romans chapter one that the Gentile world
was without excuse when it came to the
existence of God. The Psalmist would

declare that the man who says there is no God is a fool. (Psa. 14:1)

The Bible is a book about how God has dealt with man and man has dealt with God throughout history. Abraham, Moses, David, Peter, John, Paul and others claim to have had experiences with God. His Son Jesus Christ came in the flesh as the greatest demonstration of both the existence of this God and what He is like. Jesus could say *"If you have seen me you have seen the Father." (John 14:9b)* In ages past, men have been burned at the stake, thrown to the lions, and yes, even crucified, rather than deny their faith in this God. When we believe this God exists and is the only God, we are in good company. I love being in good company. "Faith" in this God truly *"is the victory that overcomes the world." (1John 5:4)* If and when we are called upon to suffer for our faith, remember we are not alone.

> *"Christ suffered for us leaving us*
> *an example that we should follow*
> *in His steps; who did no sin,*
> *neither was guile found in His*

7

mouth; who, when He was reviled, reviled not again; when He suffered, threatened not; but committed himself to Him that judges righteously.
(1Pet 2:21-23)

This is our perfect example in suffering. Hebrews chapter eleven gives a long list of those who for their faith:

"...some faced jeers and flogging, while still others were chained and put in prison. They were stoned; they were sawed in two; they were put to death by the sword. They went about in sheepskins and goat skins, destitute; persecuted and mistreated — the world was not worthy of them"
(Heb 11:36-37) NIV

It is said that when the heathens saw how the early Christian were willing to die for their faith they were moved to believe. They reasoned there must be something to this if

8

these are willing to die rather than deny their God.

There is a story from one of the wars where a woman and her brother were chased down a street and into a blind alley where the brother was killed. The woman escaped. Later she was working in a military hospital when the soldier who had killed her brother was brought in as a wounded prisoner. She was faced with a decision; she could very easily let him die. But she gave him the best care she could and he recovered. He recognized the woman and asked her why she would do such a thing; why she did not just let him die. She answered "I am a follower of the One who commanded us to love our enemies and do them good." The soldier was silent for a while and then he spoke: "I never knew there was such a religion as this, tell me more about it. What this woman believed about this God made the difference in her actions.

I experienced this personally. A young mother, a member of our congregation in Michigan, was dying with cancer. I was visiting with her in the hospital. She was so calm and at peace and had been talking with some of the other patients. She knew she was dying and talked openly about it. A teenage girl was in a bed close by who was about to have her first operation and she was scared. I talked with her and she remarked how she had never been put to sleep and it was scary. She said, "I wish I had whatever that woman has." She did not know what being a Christian was about; all she knew was she would like to have the calm assurance this woman who was dying with cancer had. I tried to assure her she could have the same. It is all because of the faith this woman had in God.

This is the God this little volume is all about. Come with me as we search for a better understanding of just who this God is and why He acts the way He does. This volume by itself will not be enough. Within the 66 books of the Bible is where you will really find the mind of this God revealed. You will find Him on every page. Allow Him to explain Himself. If you have fallen in love with Him, I hope that love will become stronger. If you have not yet fallen in love with Him, I hope you won't be able to resist.

Chapter Two

Incomprehensible

*"Oh the depth of the riches of the
wisdom and knowledge of God! How
unsearchable His judgments and His
paths beyond tracing out! Who has
known the mind of the Lord? Or who
has been His counselor? Who has ever
given to God, that God should repay
Him? For from Him and through Him
and to Him are all things. To Him be
the glory forever! Amen.*

(Rom 11:33-36)

Some Bible Publishers list this as the doxology of the apostle Paul in that chapter to the Romans which most admit is difficult to comprehend. On the heels of this statement, he gives perhaps the greatest discourses on Christian living ever recorded. *Rom.12* My father used to say, "Every area of the Christian faith is covered in this chapter."

I like the words of Eliphaz when he was giving a reply to what Job had said in a previous chapter. He says:

> *"But if it were I, I would appeal to God; I would lay my cause before Him. He performs wonders that cannot be fathomed, miracles that cannot be counted."*
> *(Job 5:8-9)*

> *"He has also set eternity in the hearts of men; yet they cannot fathom what God has done from beginning to end."*
> *(Ecc 3:11b)*

13

Speaking to Israel through Isaiah, God must have thought they needed to be reminded that He is above and beyond, when He said:

"For My thoughts are not your thoughts, nor are your ways My ways," says the LORD. "For as the heavens are higher than the earth, so are My ways higher than your ways and My thoughts than your thoughts."

(Isa 55:8-9)

When we begin any endeavor we need to understand what our limitations are. This is extremely important as we engage in this endeavor. Here we are dealing with someone who is so far beyond us it is sometimes scary to try to think in His terms. From the outset it requires humility on our part. Perhaps this is why Jesus would start that great sermon from the mount the way He did. *"Blessed are the poor in spirit for theirs is the kingdom of heaven." (Matt.5:1)*

The true God is beyond our ability to

comprehend: We are finite beings, (so limited) trying to deal with One who is infinite (without limits). It is fitting that we come on our knees. For this reason alone, we could never completely understand Him.

This is where we must trust Him completely to reveal to us just enough that we can comprehend and make a part of our lives. He has made us. He knows just how much we can take in. He knows just how much we need to have complete faith. When we have taken in the limit, He has revealed we can have faith to trust the things we cannot know to Him. Paul understood this when he wrote,

> *"Everyone who calls on the name of the Lord will be saved. How, then, can they call on the one they have not believed in? and how can they believe in the one of whom they have not heard? And how can they hear without someone preaching to them?*
> *(Rom.10:13-15)*

In this undertaking we pray:

Oh God. Because Your ways are not our ways and Your thoughts are not our thoughts we humbly acknowledge our total dependence on You for any knowledge about who You really are. Unless You guide us we wander aimlessly in our search. Without You to say "Peace be still" the storm would consume us. Help us to know there are things we need not and cannot know, so when we have gone as far as our finite understanding permits, in faith sustain us and let us be content with the revelation You have given and love You in response. We ask in and by the Name of the One who showed us best what You are really like. Amen.

As a child, most of us have asked, "Where did God come from?" Later a little more mature in our thinking we are almost sure to ask the question, "What is God like?" If we try to answer this question from our own human perception, we are sure to muddy the waters. We must allow God himself to supply the answer. This is because He is not like anything or anyone we might imagine in our own mind.

"Canst thou by searching find out God?"
Was the question asked by Zophar the Naamathite.
"Canst thou find out the Almighty unto perfection? It is high as the heaven; what canst thou do? Deeper than hell; what canst thou know?"
(Job 11:7-8)

"No one knows the Father except the Son," said our Lord, *"and those to whom the Son will reveal Him."* John's gospel reveals the helplessness of lowly man to fathom the mysteries of God. Paul tells us that the mind of God can only be revealed by the Spirit of God and known by man with a seeking heart that is open.

So whatever, with our finite minds, we visualize God to be, we can rest assured He is not. For anything we could imagine would be like something He has created and the first commandment forbids the making of anything that would resemble anything that was made. If we insist on trying to imagine Him, we risk ending up with an idol, made not with hands but with

17

thoughts; and an idol formed in the mind is no better or less offensive than an idol made from wood or stone.

I have heard some say "The Bible is too hard to understand and I just don't try. I'll leave it to those who go to the seminary to understand it." One man said, "I pay my priest good money to study for me." Surely his priest would advise him otherwise.

This God came nearest when He was incarnated in human flesh. When He went to the cross, He made the perfect atonement that made reconciliation possible for all and with outstretched arms He says, I love you this much. When He arose from the grave, the hope for eternal life became real for obedient believers. Oh sure, there are still mysteries, but we now have enough to take hold and hang on with all our might.

Throughout Scripture when men have come close to the presence of this God they are always so overwhelmed they usually fall to their knees. Moses at the burning bush was told, *"Take your sandals off your feet, for the place where you stand is holy ground". (Ex3:5b)* When Isaiah came into the temple and saw the Lord high and lifted up, the best he could say was *"Woe is me."* *(Isa.6:5a)* In the Psalm chapter fifty, God reminds the Psalmist of some of the things the people were doing and thinking they would get away with, and God knows the reason they were thinking this way, He says:

> *"These things you have done and I kept silent: you thought that I was altogether like you: but I will rebuke you, and set them in order before your eyes."*
> *(Ps 50:21-22)*

Man, left to his own thinking and work, will be tempted at least to try and reduce God to manageable terms. Man would like to get God down to where he can use Him, at least to know where He is if and when he needs Him. Man desires a god that in some measure he can control. He would like a god who would keep his distance but come running when he calls. Man wants the feeling of security that comes from thinking he knows what God is like. What He is like may be nothing more than the sum of a group of pictures we have seen; or people we have known or heard about; and all the great ideas we have entertained. Imagining a god like this may give us good feelings just like reading a fairy tale story to a child may help them to fall asleep, but that's all it is.

If all this sounds strange to our ears, it may very well be that we have for too long taken God for granted. He may very well be nothing more than what we have created in our minds. The true glory of this God has not been really taught to our generation. Our children have been left to create a god in their mind that they are comfortable with. Satan has taken full advantage of this failure and encouraged man in inventing a god just a little superior to us humans, and we tell ourselves we are not idolaters. Such a god is not sufficient to command the total surrender of our lives.

If what we have conceived God to be He is not, then how shall we think of Him? If He indeed is incomprehensible, and He declares Himself to be; if He is unapproachable, as Paul says He is, how can the hunger that burns deep within us be satisfied? How shall we come to know One who eludes all the efforts of our mind and heart? And how shall we be held accountable to know that which cannot be known? This, at first, may seem like an unsolvable mystery but nowhere has God ever held man accountable for that which he cannot know. No such charge can ever be brought against this God.

The yearning to know what cannot be known; to comprehend the Incomprehensible; to touch and taste the Unapproachable; surely comes from that image of our Creator that is a part of our nature and sets us apart from the animal kingdom. Though man is limited by all the things which make him human, deep in his soul is a desire to know his origin and return to his source. This is part of that threefold question "Where did I come from? "Why am I here?" and, "Where am I going?" One ancient writer has said, "There is a longing in the heart of every man that

21

can never be satisfied until he finds his source and that source is God." In the midst of this with all our questions we need to realize, yes, we must admit, our dependence on Him to reveal Himself.

The answer is found in the Bible and the most complete revelation in that book is found in the person and life of Jesus Christ who is a part of the Godhead himself. He has shown himself sufficient that we can believe with all our heart and love with all our being. God came near us when He was incarnated in human flesh. When He died once and for all making atonement for our sins, He made forgiveness and recon- ciliation possible for all. When He came forth in His resurrection, He brought hope of life and immortality beyond this life within the reach of us all. Through an obedient faith, we can enter and confidently lay hold on Him. No, we don't totally understand Him, but with faith based on that which He has revealed, we hold on with all our might.

Someone may ask. "If we cannot fully understand this God, then why not just forget about even trying?" The answer is, though we may not be able to fully comprehend, there is sufficient evidence we can know to cause us to love Him and respond in a worthy fashion. Look at it this way: in climbing a mountain you may never reach the top but the higher you climb the greater will be the view. In fact this is one of the wonderful things about God; this tells us He is above us; He is worthy of our worship and adoration; He is not just a man; He is God. If we could perfectly comprehend Him, then He would be too small for God!

So, you are disappointed because there are some things you don't understand about Him, don't be. Trust Him, and glory in the wonder of that portion He has chosen to reveal. I assure you, He has given us all we can stand. There is all our finite mind can work with during this life and if we trust Him we will see Him face to face in eternity. *"When this mortal shall have put on immortality; when this corruption shall have put on incorruption."* Then our faith will become sight. Those who accepted what was revealed and placed their trust and hope in Him, who is above and beyond us, will be so overwhelmed with His glory it will take an eternity to praise Him enough.

But as it is written:

> *"Eye has not seen, nor ear heard, nor have entered into the heart of man the things which God has prepared for those who love Him. But God has revealed them to us through His Spirit. For the Spirit searches all things, yes, the deep things of God. For what man knows the things of a man except the spirit of the man which is in him? Even so no one knows the things of God except the Spirit of God.*
> *(1Cor 2:9-11)*

Just how much do we need to know about this God? Will there ever be a time when, "enough is enough?" God must have decided we needed to know what He revealed about himself, this is why He did it. I don't think anyone needs worry about knowing too much. When we have absorbed

24

all that has been revealed, and our mind has been challenged to its limit, there will still be plenty to wonder about and revealed in eternity.

We need the humility of heart and absence of all prejudices. We need no ax to grind; no preconceived ideas or dogmas to defend. We will not have to read His revelation very far to begin to see enough of this God to know He is worthy and by every right should command our full allegiance.

William Cowper said it so well:
  "God moves in a mysterious way,
    His wonders to perform;
  He plants His footsteps in the sea,
    and rides upon the storm.
  Deep in unfathomable minds,
    of never failing skill,
  He treasures up His bright designs,
    and works His gracious will.
  Ye fearful saints, fresh courage take,
    the clouds ye so much dread.
    are big with mercy,
  and shall break in blessings on your head.

25

His purposes will ripen fast,
unfolding every hour;
The bud may have a bitter taste,
but sweet will be the flower.
Blind unbelief is sure to err,
and scan His work in vain;
God is His own interpreter,
and He will make it plain."

And, **THAT'S GOOD NEWS!**

Chapter Three

ONE GOD IN THREE PERSONS

*Then God said, "Let **us** make man in our image, according to **our** likeness." (Gen 1:26a)*

*"For there are **three** who bear witness in heaven: the **Father**, the **Word**, and the **Holy Spirit**; and these **three** agree as one."*
(1Jn 5:7)

*"And without controversy great is the mystery of godliness: **God** was manifest in the **flesh,** justified in the **Spirit**, seen of angels, preached unto the Gentiles, believed on in the world, received up into glory."*
(1Tim 3:16)

*"How much more shall the blood of **Christ**, who through the **eternal Spirit** offered Himself without spot **to God,** purge your conscience from dead works to serve the living **God?"** (Heb 9:14)*

*"Elect according to the foreknowledge of God
the **Father**, through sanctification of the **Spirit,**
unto obedience and sprinkling of the blood of
Jesus Christ: Grace unto you, and
peace, be multiplied." (I Pe 1:2)*

"I and my Father are one."
(Jn 10:30)

Anytime we try and think of a being that is infinite, we are stretching the outer limits of our finite abilities. When we try to wrap our minds around the idea of "three in one", we are forced to admit this is too high; we cannot reach this far. Some, because the actual word "Trinity" is not found in scripture, have rejected any teaching that uses the word. A difficult thing for the finite mind of man to try and comprehend is that attribute of God which we call the "Trinity." Yes, there are things about the Trinity that are beyond our understanding. However, this is true of all His attributes.

The idea of a triune God is abundant throughout scripture. The writers make little effort to explain it. God's Spirit must have known it could not be explained to our finite minds. So, it is just stated and left at that. Just as Adam and Eve were not satisfied with God's simple instructions in the

28

garden, modern man is not satisfied with God's simple statements that He is "Three in One."

This effort is in no way trying to explain any more from God's side but only trying to get us, as His creatures, to accept what He has revealed and to glory in it. The Trinity, as with all His attributes, shows the wonder of this God we serve. Instead of being discouraged and turned away, we allow it to draw us to Him. Any God we could fully understand would be too small and a god that small would not command our full commitment. So let us rejoice that He is above us and beyond us. Yes, those looking for a god they can control and manipulate will find themselves disappointed with this Triune God. He is above us and beyond us. We cannot reach that high. However, we can rejoice that He has graciously revealed enough of Himself for the human mind to grasp and to love. That is sufficient. Our task is to reach for that which He has chosen to reveal and hold on with all our might.

Because we are treading on such holy ground, and our best efforts will fall so short, we must be extremely careful less we are found guilty of presumption. This is not an option God has given us.

Those who reject what they cannot explain

have denied the Trinity because it does not agree with their human reasoning. They conclude it is impossible for Him to be both one and three. There are so many mysteries all around us. Life itself is surrounded with mysteries we can't explain. Then why should we have such difficulty acknowledging that God would be beyond our comprehension.

Every person lives every day to some degree by faith, the non-believer as well as the believer; the one lives by faith in the natural laws and the other by faith in God. Why don't we just admit we all accept things we do not fully understand?

We use some of the energy that rushes through our world. We have it at our finger tips. It works for us and we enjoy it. But so little of it we understand. In our pride we are ashamed and hesitant to admit there just might be some mystery that we, in our finite stage, cannot understand.

The church has repeated the Scriptures that set forth the Trinity. Some have tried to explain it, but the more man tries to explain things that are unexplainable the more confusing it becomes. Perhaps some things just need to be stated, believed, and then left alone.

I'm reminded of the story of the teacher who was asking pupils for their homework assignment. One little boy said, "Teacher, I don't have my home work. I forgot it and left it at home." Another said, "We had company, and when they left, I fell asleep." One little girl said, "The dog ate mine." Finally, he asked the last little boy named Johnny, "Why do you not have your homework?" Johnny answered, "I'm sorry teacher, but I don't think I can add anything to what has already been said."

Some deny the Trinity on the grounds that the whole concept contradicts the idea of one God. They see the idea of Trinity being three gods, not one God in three persons. The Bible declares over and over, "there is one God", and it declares there are three in the Godhead. Read and ponder the words of Philippians 2:-6-11. Speaking of Jesus, the writer declares, *"Who being in very nature God, did not consider equality with God something to be held on to but made himself nothing, taking the very nature of a servant, being made in human likeness."* Take that statement along with John 1. The Word was in the beginning with God and that Word was God. They are God. They are one. Jesus claimed, *"I and my Father are one."* I can almost hear Him say, "Trust Me."

To the humble heart that is sufficient, but to the proud heart that demands an explanation that satisfies all its whims, will not only reject this but will question the other attributes of God as well.

God through all eternity is the Triune God. He did not start out with just one person and sometime later the other two were added. There are some who try to say that Jesus was created somewhere along the way by God who called Him His Son. This false concept has led to other erroneous teachings. There is one group that teaches that there is only one in the Godhead and his name is Jesus. This they say is the only name that can be applied to God. They go so far as to teach that baptism can only be done in the name of Jesus. Baptism in the name of the Father, Son, and Holy Spirit is invalid because it adds to the name of God which is Jesus. Remember, we said earlier that every false doctrine can be traced to some erroneous concept of God.

What if Abraham had refused to obey until God explained how he was going to work everything out after Isaac was sacrificed? There might never have been a nation of Israel. The scripture declares that Abraham, against all the evidence *"waxed strong in faith, giving glory to God."* Anselm, who some call "the second Augustine," held that faith must precede all effort to understand. I cannot accept that without some reservation, but certainly we do reach a point that all we have is faith. But that faith is not blind. It is based upon that which has been revealed. We believe the things that have been revealed, and we trust Him in those things which have not been fully revealed, that He will make even that known in His own time.

Peter speaks of that day we *"receive the end of our faith, the salvation of our souls." (1Pet.1:9)* Until that day we say, *"Let God be true and every man a liar."* One reason you can know it's true. There is a Godhead made up of three in one in a bond of unity that is beyond our comprehension, This one God existing in three persons has always been. He has no beginning and no end. He has never been any different than He is now and will ever be. He changes not! He is the One who said it. When we don't have first hand knowledge of something, we are forced to take the word of someone else. We believe or disbelieve based on the credibility of the one who said it. Friends, this Triune God has plenty of credibility.

The doctrine of the Trinity is a doctrine to be believed but not to be fully understood. Anselm pleaded, *"Let me seek Thee in longing. Let me long for Thee in seeking; let me find Thee in love, and love Thee in finding."* Faith in such a God is not blind but rest on solid ground and we can love Him because He first loved us. Our human pride will have to take a back seat.

Jesus seemed happy to use the plural form when

speaking of Himself along with the Father and Spirit. *"We will come to Him and make our abode with Him."* He boldly declared, *"I and My Father are one."* Yes, it is important that we think of our God as "three in one", in perfect unity. There has never been a disagreement among the three. The substance cannot be divided. Yes, to think in a manner worthy of such a God is a noble task that should not to be taken lightly.

Remember, it was Jesus' claim to be equal with the Father that so outraged the religious leaders of his day and led to his crucifixion. When Jesus claimed to be equal with God, the Jews said He was guilty of blasphemy. If He was guilty of blasphemy, then He could be put to death legally. This may be why for the most part the Jewish people have never made any apology for their part in the crucifixion. As a blasphemer, He would have been worthy of death. The early church fathers understood this as being fundamental to the Christian faith. When a group of those church fathers met in Nicaea two centuries later and adopted a statement of their belief it reads:

> I believe in one Lord Jesus Christ,
> The only begotten Son of God,
> Begotten of Him before all ages,
> God of God, light of light,
> Very God of very God,

Begotten, not made,
> Being of one substance with the Father,
> By whom all things were made.

This statement says in a nutshell what our faith is in. Some today might word it a little different, but basically it stands true. They felt just as strong that the Spirit was also a equal part of the Godhead. This statement sets forth this belief in very bold terms as well.

> I believe in the Holy Spirit
> The Lord and giver of life,
> Which proceeded from the Father?
> And the Son,
> Who with the Father and Son
> Together is worshiped and glorified.

When Jesus walked the earth, He spoke to the Father and the Father answered Him. In His prayer in John chapter seventeen, He prays that the Father would restore Him to the glory He had with Him before the world was. We are told that He now intercedes with the Father for us at the Father's right hand. That perfect communion between the Godhead has existed from all eternity and knows no bounds. We might argue that communion was broken for a moment when it seems the Father withdrew his presence when the Son was taking the place of the sinner. *(Mk 15:34)* Even there it can be said the Father and Spirit were participating. I am convinced much of the confusion has come by trying to separate the Three. The Jews claimed they believed God the Father but would not accept Jesus. Jesus made it plain, that the one who rejects Him was rejecting the One that sent Him, and the one that receives Him receives the One that sent Him. *Mk 10:40, Jn 13:20*

A popular belief among some Christians today would divide the work of the Godhead among the three entities, saying each has a specific part. For instance, the work of creation is attributed to the Father; the work of redemption is attributed to the Son; and regeneration is attributed to the Spirit. This may be true in part but not wholly so. The problem with this is that it would put each of the Godhead in a box; they can only go so far and then the other has to take over and carry on. God cannot be divided up so that one part works while another is inactive. Rather, they all work in perfect unity at all time. What one does, they all do. What one says, they all say. Some of the confusion about the work of the Holy Spirit is the result of this thinking.

The work of creation is attributed to the Father (Gen.1:1), to the Son *(Col.1:16),* and to the Spirit *(Job.26:13* and *Psa. 104:30).* The incarnation is

36

shown to have been accomplished by the three Persons in full accord *(Lk.1:35)*, though only the Son became flesh to dwell among us. At Jesus' baptism, the Son came up out of the water, the Spirit descended and the Father spoke from heaven *(Matt.3:16-17)*. A beautiful description is found in Hebrews *9:14*, which states *that Christ, through the eternal Spirit, offered Himself without spot to God.* Again, we see the three Persons operating together.

The resurrection of Christ is attributed to the Father *(Acts 2:32),* to the Son *(Jn 10:17-18),* and to the Holy Spirit *(Rom.1:4).* The salvation of man is shown to be the work of all three. *(1Pet.1:2).* And the indwelling in the soul of man is shown to be by the Father, the Son, and the Holy Spirit *(Jn 14:15-23).*

Such a wonderful truth as this had to be revealed. The fallen mind of man would never have imagined such. Even revealed in such splendor, it is still difficult for man to accept simply because it does not fit into his mold of thinking. Sometimes his pride gets in the way.

In the presence of this Holy Triune God, every living creature falls down and worships. *Rev 4, 5*

One verse of the old song entitled
"Holy! Holy! Holy!

Holy, holy, holy! Lord God Almighty!
All Thy works shall praise Thy name,
In earth, and sky, and sea;
Holy, holy, holy! merciful and mighty!
God in three Persons, blessed Trinity.
(Reginald Heber}

And, **THAT'S GOOD NEWS!**

Chapter Four

THE GOD OF LIFE

"And the Lord God formed man of the dust of the ground, and breathed into his nostrils the breath of life: and man became a living being." *(Gen 2:7)*

"In Him was life, and the life was the light of men."
(John 1:4)

Man is at war with God over one thing: who will be in control of life? Every sin is rooted in this struggle. The war will only cease when man makes the unconditional surrender.

When Moses stood before Pharaoh and told him that God said, *"Let my people go,"* Pharaoh asked Moses *"who is this god?"* Pharaoh was thinking in terms of just another god, perhaps a little different from the many gods the Egyptians worshipped. He was by no means ready to concede any authority to another god beyond the gods he was acquainted with. He had his own magicians which were able to demonstrate some of the powers he would attribute to one of his gods. This God through Moses was going to demonstrate to Pharaoh and all Egypt that there was an unmistakable difference in this God and the gods of the Egyptians. When that night in Egypt has passed, Pharaoh and the entire world would have no problem knowing who the true God is and who is not.

God through Moses and Aaron went through a series of nine plagues, after which it should have been clear enough. But Pharaoh would resist and his stubborn heart would not give in. God had told Moses in advance this would happen. Then God spoke to Moses:

"And the Lord said to Moses, I will bring one more plague on Pharaoh and on Egypt. Afterward he will let you go from here. When he does, he will drive you out completely"

(Ex 11:1)

After nine plagues on his nation, Pharaoh's heart was still hardened. The deciding battle between the true God and the false gods of Egypt was about to take place. What was about to happen would be an event that would be remembered by these people throughout future generations. It would be so significant it would become the center piece of worship for them. It would be called "The Passover". This event would also serve as a type (shadow) of a future day when God Himself would offer a Lamb (His Son) on a hill outside Jerusalem for the sins of the whole world. Sacrifices had been offered all the way back to Cain and Able, but this was special. The Israelites would reenact this event once each year as a reminder of how their God had delivered them from bondage and it would stand as a testimony to the Egyptian people and the world if they would only take notice.

41

Very special instructions were given in preparation for this event. They were instructed to kill the lamb which had been selected for this purpose, and kept separate from the other sheep. They were to prepare the meat a special way, eat the meat, burn the leftovers and sprinkle the blood of the lamb on the door post of their homes as a sign. God promised when He saw the blood He would Passover and not take the firstborn of that house. God continued:

> *"About midnight I will go out into the midst of Eqypt: and all the firstborn in the land of Eqypt will die, from the firstborn of Pharaoh who sits on the throne, even to the firstborn of the maidservant who is behind the hand mill, and all the firstborn of the beasts. Then there shall be a great cry throughout all the land of Egypt, such as was not like it before, nor shall be like it again. But against none of the children of Israel shall a dog move its tongue: against man or beast, that you may know that the Lord makes a difference between the Egyptians and Israel." (Ex 11:4b-7)*

When this plague was finished there would be no doubt in Pharaoh's mind just who this God is. He would be more than glad to let these people go. When the clock struck midnight the cry such as had never been heard before, and would never be heard again echoed throughout Egypt, Pharaoh awakened and went to the room of his firstborn and found him dead.

> *"For there was not a house where there was not one dead."*   *(Ex 12:30b)*

Notice, this was not some kind of a hit-miss operation. If you were lucky your family would not be hit with this plague. In every house from the king's palace down to the lowest peasant, the life of the firstborn was taken.

Genesis declared that *"God formed man of the dust of the ground and breathed into his nostrils the breath of life, and man became a living being."* This has always been the deciding factor between the would-be gods and the true God, the one who controls life must be the ONE.

The Bible is a book about life and the God that gives life. There was a country song a few years ago that said, *"It's my life let me live it like I please."* We just don't want anyone interfering with our life. I fear too many people feel this way about God. God leave me alone; it's my life; I think I should be allowed to live it the way I think will make me happy. All the way through the Bible God is crying out to mankind, "I have made you. I gave you life. I created for you the good things, not bad things. I have given you free choice but I want you to choose the good. And the choice you make will have eternal consequences".

God calls out to us:

> *"See now that I, even I, am Me: and there is no god with Me: I kill, and I make alive; I wound, and I heal; nor is there any that can deliver out of My hand." (Deut 32:39)*

When Jesus was here He had great difficulty convincing the Jews that He was God. He gave three demonstrations which should have convinced them:

He raised the little maid who had died.
(*Lk 8:51-55*)

He raised the son of the woman in Nain.
(Lk 11:7-15)
After His friend Lazarus had been dead for four days, when Jesus called his name, Lazarus came out of the tomb alive. *(Jn 11:21-44)*

Then, to climax it all, He went to the grave Himself, stayed three days and came out alive. Let it forever be known, HE IS THE GOD OF LIFE!

In the face of all the evidence it is sad the very people who had been the greatest recipients of this God's special blessings, still for the most part reject the One who came to save them.

Because he is the God of Life, His Word declares:

"Be not deceived, God is not mocked; for whatever a man sows, that he will also reap. For he who sows to the flesh will of the flesh reap corruption, but he who sows to the Spirit will of the Spirit reap life everlasting." (Gal 6:8-9)

God is sovereign. And to be sovereign He must be sovereign over all; and to be sovereign over all, He must be in control of life. If there was one life

He did not have final control over He would not be God. If He is sovereign over my life that means He owns me. So it's not my life to live as I please. Yes, I may live the way I please, but rest assured there will be consequences. Jesus could say...

"for every idle word man will give account."
(Matt 12:36)

Our generation struggles with abortion and can't seem to figure out if it's right or wrong. Man considers himself so smart, but he can't agree when life begins. He seems to think as long as he doesn't know when life begins then he is innocent if he ends it. One side thinks Science should prove it then the government could pass a law and settle it. I doubt that will happen to satisfy very many. We don't seem to be able to decide if we can take our own life or not. Why not, if I don't feel like living, what could be wrong with it? If I see my loved one suffering, why can't I pull the plug?

All of these are basic questions about life and can only be answered with an understanding of who has control of life. Science will never discover the answer in a laboratory and all the decisions handed down by the Supreme Court cannot answer the question.

Man is at war with God over one thing, which

will be in control of life. Every sin is rooted in this struggle. The war will only cease when man makes the unconditional surrender. We must let God be God. This peace cannot be negotiated.

Job knew very well who has the sovereign right over life. When his wife saw him suffering so much it may well have been out of compassion that she said *"Why don't you just curse God and die."* Job replied:

"The Lord gives and the Lord takes
away and blessed be His name."
(Job 2:10)

This is a lesson I fear modern man has yet to learn. This God gives and He takes away which is His sovereign right. This is the reason the penalty for murder was so severe in the Old Testament. Man who would take another life has usurped the role of God and by doing so had forfeited his own life. Some have misunderstood some of God's actions. He put people to death for reasons our modern society would consider trivial because it thinks it has the right to decide what just punishment is. In this they fail to recognize that God is the God of life and He alone has that right. We must give way to His sovereignty. His right over life is not up for negotiation. God is not being unreasonable when He asks us to submit our lives to His will.

Rather than cause us problems, let us rejoice that the One who made us and gives us life is in control. If He did not have the final say, we would really be in trouble. He loves us and wants us to have *"life abundantly"* here and *"eternal life"* in the world to come. Because He is the God of life He can say:

> *"Verily, verily, I say to you, he who hears My words and believes on Him that sent Me has everlasting life, and shall not come into judgment but has passed from death into life. Most assuredly, I say to you, the hour is coming when the dead will hear the voice of the Son of God, and those who hear will live. For the father has life in Himself, so He has granted the Son to have life in Himself Do not marvel at this, for the hour is coming in which all who are in the graves will hear His voice and come forth those who have done good to the resurrection of life, and those who have done evil to the*

48

resurrection of condemnation."
(Jn 5:24-25,28-29)

Because He is the God of life He can promise, and we can believe:

"I am the resurrection and the life. He who believes in Me though he may die, he shall live. And whoever lives and believes in Me shall never die."
(Jn 11:25-26)

Paul was well aware of whom he was speaking when he stood among the philosophers in Athens and declared:

"Therefore, the One whom you worship without knowing Him I proclaim to you: God, who made the world and everything in it, since He is Lord of heaven and earth, does not dwell in temples made with hands. Nor is he worshipped with men's hands as though He needed anything, since He gives to all life, breath, and all things. And He has made from one blood every nation of men to dwell on all the face of the

49

earth, and has determined their pre-appointed times and the boundaries of their habitation. So that they should seek the Lord, in the hope that they might grope for Him and find Him, though He is not far from each one of us: for in Him we live and move and have our being, as also some of your own poets have said, "For we are also His offspring." Therefore, since we are the offspring of God, we ought not to think that the Divine Nature is like gold or silver or stone, something shaped by art and man's devising. Truly, these times of ignorance God overlooked, but now commands all men everywhere to repent, because He has appointed a day on which He will judge the world in righteousness by the Man whom He has ordained. He has given assurance of this to all by raising Him from the dead." (Acts 17:23-31)

Because He is the God of life He can promise, and we can believe:

"I am the resurrection and the life. He who believes in Me though he die, he shall live. And whoever lives and believes in Me shall never die. Do you believe this?"(Jn 11: 25-26).

There is no more peaceful scene than a newborn baby resting in the arms of its mother who has just given birth. But sweeter yet it will be when the child of God will rest eternally safe in the arms of the One who gave us life and laid down His own life to give us eternal life. Fanny Crosby's words are assuring and express the hope of every true believer: *"Safe in the arms of Jesus, safe on His gentle breast, there by His love o'er shaded, sweetly my soul shall rest".* Jesus has assured the faithful on His right hand that they *"will go away into everlasting life."* (Matt 25:46b)

In Revelation chapter twenty, John saw a book in heaven being opened that contained the names of these who will live eternally with God. And that book is called the "BOOK OF LIFE". In this age of the World Wide Web and e-mail, I think my name must be in a thousand lists around the world. But to have my name in that book is the most important. This hope is the "anchor of the soul" that keeps us going when the going gets tough.

This is not just academic. It is relevant to our everyday life. We need the assurance that the One who controls life is able and will sustain us. It's good to know we are not aimlessly drifting through this life without a destination in mind, but our life is safe within His hands. Without that hope our life would be hopeless indeed.

When that saint who had been persecuted from all sides, and was waiting to be put to death for the cause he had once persecuted: from his prison cell could pen these words:

> *"For this reason I also suffer these things; nevertheless I am not shamed, for I know whom I have believed and am persuaded that His is able to keep what I have committed to Him until that day."*
> *(II Tim 1:12)*

> *"For I am already being poured out as a drink offering, and the time of my departure is at hand. I have fought the good fight, I have finished the race, I have kept the faith. Finally, there is laid up for me the crown of righteous-*

ness, which the Lord, the righteous Judge, will give to me on the day, and not to me only but also to all who have loved His appearing."

(II Tim 4:6-8)

And, **THAT'S GOOD NEWS!**

Chapter Five

SELF-EXISTENT

*"In the beginning was the Word, and the Word
was with God, and the Word was God."*
(Jn 1:1)

*"And God said to Moses, I AM WHO I AM;
and He said, thus you shall say to the children of
Israel, 'I AM has sent me to you.'"*
(Ex 3:14)

If God is in the beginning, and according to Genesis one He is; if nothing else existed then, He of necessity is self-existent. There is still so much man does not know about our universe but we have learned that everything is dependent on something else to some extent. Man is not self-existent but is dependent on a great number of things for support. Man's exploration of space is to a large degree a search for things that would support life and so far he has not found another planet with sufficient resources to support life. This is not to say these do not exist, but we do know human life is not self-existent.

Perhaps this is one reason the atheist and skeptic do not want to admit the existence of God, they would be forced to admit He is self-existent. That would make us dependent on Him for our existence and that the atheist and skeptic does not seem willing to do. So, this characteristic of God is very basic to a working faith.

Wycliffe has this to say in his commentary on the first verse of Genesis:

> *"God is the creator of all things. From the outset in the book of Genesis, the focus of the strong light of revelation*

turns upon the Almighty. He is the beginning, the cause, the source of all that is. He brought into being all things and the persons that were to fit into his plan for the ages. All the matter necessary for his later working, he miraculously created."

Paul told the Greek philosophers in Athens that this God, unknown to them, did not need anything from them. Their life had come from Him. This probably came as a surprise. Man, in his pride, would like to think of himself as a stand alone. In some cases he would like for God to just leave him alone and let him do it his way. I think someone had a song about "doing it my way," didn't he? One of the fast food chains had a slogan that said *"Have it your way."*

This is why an idol is such an offense to the true God. An idol is something that is made by someone and without that someone the idol would not exist. In this way we can know the difference between would-be gods and the true God.

We are sometimes reluctant to do something for someone who we think does not need it. This is one of those times when we get more than we give. We give to Him of our time and talents and He doesn't need any of them. He multiplies our blessings in return. This is why everything we do in service to Him is for our own good. Perhaps this is one reason at least we are told, *"It is more blessed to give than to receive."*

We hear a lot of talk about the Origin of the Universe. Man spends a lot of time and money trying to find out just when and how it came into being. When we look at something, it is almost natural to ask, "Where did it come from and how did it get here?" It is not strange man would try to trace things back to a beginning. The believer has no objection to this. We get back to the beginning, and there is God. He is the self-existent, self-sufficient source. The atheist says, "No, it's all just by chance." But then they keep searching trying to find something to replace the chance. We have the sufficient source and have no need to look for a replacement.

When children ask us questions about God, "where did He come "from?" etc., don't make up a lot of fairy tale stuff because we think they will not understand. Tell them the truth. I know they will not fully understand, but later when they do they will be glad. Many have been told fairy tales and now are in need of being re-taught. There is so much more to the Bible than a story of a big flood and a ark full of animals; a host of people walking across a river on dry land; a big fish that swallowed a man for three days; a little boy who killed a big giant with a little stone and a sling; even feeding five thousand with loaves and fish; or turning water into wine. All these are interesting stories but they need to see the big God who is working through it all. He wants and deserves to have complete control of our lives. They need to know He is able to give us abundant life here and eternal life. He gave His Son to make it possible. If we fail in this, we could just as well have told them fairy tales for sure.

Yes, there is a God who exists outside all our understandings. He needs nothing from any of us, certainly not advice or help in judging others. He will not appear before our courts of human reason to answer our questions which we have no right to ask in the first place. It is painful to admit that we need everything and He needs nothing and everything we need is something He alone can supply. Our only hope is to come before Him with open hands and humble hearts. Out of His abundant, overflowing storehouse of grace He will give us everything we need.

They tell us that our country has over spent so much that we now have to borrow forty cents of every dollar we spend. This government is still promising to give people more and more. I personally don't have much faith in a promise of something that the person has to get by borrowing from someone else. There is no way this God can promise so much that He would not have sufficient to make good His promise. This gives us great assurance. The foundation of our faith is solid. It is not because our faith is so strong, but because the object of our faith is self-existent.

Jesus who is an equal part of the self-existent Trinity said:

"Without Me you can do nothing." (Jn 15:5)

I love the way John begins his gospel. Matthew and Luke gave us the nativity scene, and it is beautiful. Mark begins his account with Jesus being baptized at the hands of John the Baptist as He begins His earthly ministry. John just seems to say let me take you back to the beginning when that eternal Word who was born in Bethlehem existed with the Father. He did not have His beginning that night in Bethlehem. This is what it's all about. This is where the rubber meets the road,

> *"In the beginning was the Word, and the Word was with God, and the Word was God. He was in the beginning with God, and without Him nothing was made that was made. In Him was life, and the life was the light of men. And the light shines in darkness, and the darkness did not comprehend it."*
> *(Jn 1:2-5)*

No greater statement could be made of the self-existence of this God. When John was closing his gospel he says there are a lot more things I could have written about but it would be too much to contain. I just want you to believe in Him and believing in Him you can have life.

He is who He says He is. He is what He says He is. He will do what He says He will do. He not only exists, He exists all by and of Himself. Nothing existed before Him and nothing will succeed Him. There is good reason John could declare:

"All things were made through Him, and without Him was nothing made that was made."

(Jn 1:3)

Jesus would proclaim from the Sermon on the Mount that the life built on faith in Him will still be standing when all the storms of life have passed by.

And, **THAT'S GOOD NEWS!**

Chapter Six

SELF-SUFFICIENT

"The God who made the world and everything in it

is the Lord of heaven and earth and does not dwell

in temples built by hands. And He is not served by

men's hands, as if He needed anything, because He

Himself gives all men life and breath

and everything else."

(Acts 17:24-26) NIV

When we talk about God's self-sufficiency, we need to be careful we are not thinking in the same realm as if we are talking about a human being's self-sufficiency. We often say he/she is self-sufficient, but we understand there are limits. But when we speak of God being self-sufficient, we mean He is totally self-sufficient. We live in a cage with limitations on every side. I personally find it difficult to think in terms of being totally self-sufficient.

Self-sufficiency is one of the all encompassing attributes on which so many other things depend. To be self-existent, He must be self-sufficient. To be sovereign, He must be self-sufficient. Simply stated, to be God, He must be self-sufficient. If by Himself He lacked anything, He would not be God.

The self-existence of God is discussed in another chapter. The two are closely connected, and many of the supporting scriptures will be the same; but, I think it is important that we understand and come to freely admit in our lives that nothing or no one is necessary to this God. If you think this is only academic, think again. We are totally dependent on God. This God existing from all eternity has never needed anything. Just because the world was created and man was made did not change the equation. He existed by Himself before there was anything else. This is why it can be said that everything that is, came from Him. John stated it in the most emphatic terms:

"Through Him all things were made;
without Him nothing was made that has
been made."
(Jn 1:3)NIV

We deal with the sovereignty of God in another chapter. His self-sufficiency is tied to His sovereignty. He can only be sovereign if He is self-sufficient. If He wills to do something, to bring it to pass He must not be dependent on someone else; He must be sufficient in Himself to accomplish the same. We seek Him not because He needs us but solely because we need Him. We love Him because He first loved us. This is the difference between this God and the gods the Athenians were worshipping.

All God is, He is in Himself. All life is in Him and comes from Him, whether it's the lowest or the highest form of life we know. Everything that is necessary to life resides in God. That means it is His right to rule our life. We have stated in another place but it bears repeating, this is why murder is wrong. This is why suicide is wrong. This is why abortion is wrong. Man is trying to assume a right to himself that belongs only to God. Even the ability to reproduce is given by God. This is why Paul could declare

> *"For in Him we live and move and have our being, as also some of your own poets have said 'For we are also His offspring.'" (Acts 17:28)*

Old Testament prophets as well as New Testament Apostles always based their teachings of right and wrong on the nature of God. It bothers me today when I hear arguments made for right or wrong based on everything but the nature of God.

God is self-sufficient in deciding right from wrong. He does not need the agreement of philosophers, psychologists or theologians. He does not need to take a poll to see if it will be acceptable with the majority. He need not call a meeting of the angels; not even the most respected church leaders are allowed to give their input to such a decision. Of the entire host mentioned in heaven, no mention is made of any group of advisors. That is why there will be no need for "assistant judges."

To admit any need would be to admit He is incomplete. Need is not a word that applies to this God. Someone may ask, why then would He be so interested in creatures like us? Why would He ask us to give to Him? Why would it make any difference whether we obeyed Him or not? In answering these questions, God is in no way trying to enrich Himself. Everything He asks from us in the end is for our benefit, not His. Down through the ages those who have responded in the affirmative will testify the end result was good for them.

Every living thing needs so much outside of self to survive. We build houses to cover us from the rain and cold. We till the ground and plant to grow our food all because we are dependent for survival. We may not have the answer for all the worlds God has created. But we can be sure they were not created to satisfy some unfulfilled need for Him.

Everything God is, He has always been. *"He is above all and through all and in you all." "He upholds all things by the word of His power."* He is not supported by the things He upholds. Did you ever wonder how the earth, sun, moon and stars can all be suspended in space with nothing visible supporting them and they never run into each other? I think we have the answer but it may take some humility to accept.

If every person on earth suddenly becomes blind, the sun would still shine by day and the moon and stars at night. These and all other planets owe nothing to us who benefit from them. So likewise if every man became an atheist, God would not be affected in any way. Man is the one who is the loser. No wonder the Bible calls the man who denies His existence a fool in Psalm.14:1.

The thought of a God who would need to court the favor of man is scary to say the least. This is why Paul did not say 'our God shall supply all your needs until He runs out of resources.' Instead he boldly declares:

> *"Our God shall supply all your needs*
> *according to His riches in glory*
> *by Christ Jesus." (Phil 4:19)*

This God is no greater because of us, and He would be no less if we did not exist. The humbling truth is we exist because of His good pleasure which we must admit is grace, not of necessity.

No where is the need for the recognition of this truth more needed than when it comes to benevolence? God is sometimes pictured as in great need of our assistance to help Him care for the needy. Some would even have you believe if you will only assist God a little bit He will repay you a hundred fold. This is almost as if He needs our help so much He is willing to pay 100 per cent interest if we will only help Him out. This is not said to take away from our need to help the unfortunate people around us, but we need to realize God has graciously given us the opportunity to share with Him and be blessed in the process. I know this doesn't make economic sense, but is another area where we trust Him for our own good, not His.

This God needs no defenders. He is always the victorious God. A god who had to depend on us who are so undependable would be an undependable god and equal to no god at all. This would be a god we could truthfully say "does not exist."

It is important and is the focus of this effort to help us rid our minds of some of these concepts of God that are so unworthy of Him. This is an effort to let Him be the God He is. Our Christian religion is about God and His dealings with man. But the main focus must be on God and not man. It must be about lifting man up to God's ideals not bringing Him down to our level. Someone says, "But did He not bring Himself down to our level in the incarnation?" Yes, that's true, but the purpose was to lift us up. He is no longer in the flesh; He now sits on the throne with everything in heaven and earth made subject to Him. Man's only claim to being any better than the beast of the field, is that he is created with the image of his creator stamped on him. The Psalmist speaks of man who:

> *"grows up like grass in the morning only to be cut down and wither. He grows up and flourishes but the wind blows and it is gone to be remembered no more." (Ps 103)*

But this God and all His attributes continue forever.

If man thinks he is so self-sufficient let him hear the beloved Peter:

> *"All flesh is as grass, and all the glory of man as the flower of the grass. The grass withers, And its flower falls away, But the word of the LORD endures forever." (I Pet 1:24-25)*

Is it any wonder scripture says faith in this God and the One who came in His Name is a must. Unbelief is a deadly sin. No created being can be allowed to trust in itself. Only this One God can trust in Himself; all others must trust in Him. The unbeliever denies the self-sufficiency of God and tries at least to usurp that roll which is not his.

This really is what the gospel is all about. This God who loved us so much that He would rather die than see us lost; not that He needed us, but without Him we would be forever lost, He disrobed Himself of His deity, and left His rightful place, and became like us, submitting Himself to all the temptations we are subject to, proving for all to see that we are without excuse. He went to that old rugged cross to pay the debt that we had nothing with which to pay. The golden text says, *"God so loved..."* That's it, He didn't just love, HE SO LOVED. That's the good news He has done for us. One thing that makes it even sweeter; He didn't have to do it but He did it anyway.

We hear a lot today about having a "relationship" with God. That's good. There's a song that talks about how "God and I walk through the fields together, we walk and talk as good friends should and do." I like that song but we must never forget this is not a "buddy, buddy" relationship. We walk together, but we are not on equal footing. It is not one of those "you scratch my back and I'll scratch yours type of relationship." He is God and I am man. He is the Master, and I am His slave. He is Lord, and I am His servant.

A few years ago there was a popular bumper sticker which read "God is my co-pilot." I remember the first one I saw, I thought was nice. But when I thought about it, I said, "That can't be right, He is supposed to be the pilot and I am not even the co-pilot; the best I can do is just ride along." I remember a flight coming back from Israel. We left Rome, came up, across Switzerland and France, and headed out across the Atlantic. The pilot came on the intercom and said, "We are headed for New York, flying at thirty six thousand feet and a speed of six hundred and fifty miles per hour. The temperature is such and such; we should be arriving at 5:20 PM New York time. I sat back and relaxed and enjoyed the ride. When the wheels hit the runway I looked at my watch and we were no more than twenty seconds off. Three hundred and sixty five passengers may have breathed a sigh of relief thinking "We made it." But we did not make it, all we did was sit in our seats and let the pilots fly the plane. I never thought for a moment that I needed to go into the cockpit and help them; in fact, that would have been a serious mistake. My help was not needed. That's the way it is with God. My help is not needed; it is not wanted; it would only mess things up so, just sit back, follow instructions, and enjoy the ride. That's how we live by faith and not by sight. This God deals with us in very simple terms that are not really that hard to understand. It does take humility on our part but for the most part it's a matter of just letting Him be God. It's all about Him not me.

And, **"That's Good News!"**

72

Chapter Seven

SUPREME

*"For the Lord is the great God; And the great
King above all gods. In His hand
are the deep places of the earth."*
(Ps 95:3-4)

*"Remember the former things of old, For I am
God, and there is no other; I am God, and there is
none like Me, declaring the end from the
beginning, and from ancient times things that are
not yet done, Saying, 'My counsel shall stand,
and I will do all My pleasure.'"*
(Isa 46:9-10)

From the first verse of Genesis to the last breath of inspiration in Revelation, the Supremacy of God runs like a vein of gold. The more I study the more I am amazed that so many people can, at least, claim they read the Bible and see everything accept God and His attributes.

I looked up the word supreme and came up with a list of things and groups who use the title of supreme; The Supreme Courts; The Supreme Court Collection; Supreme Brands; Supreme Sports; there was a singing group called The Supremes. It seems all of these want to give the impression they are the greatest in their special area. None of these groups are supreme in the same way as when it is applied to God. There are limits on each of these. The Supreme Court is only supreme for the present. Another Supreme Court in the future may overturn their decision. When we say this God is supreme that's the end of the matter. Everything about Him is eternal in duration and to the infinite degree.

Another term is used in Colossians chapter one. Paul says *"that in all things Christ should be pre-eminent."* This term means first place. We might think this is a lot like supreme, but first place is His position because He is supreme. Supreme is not just first place. The two must not be confused as the same. Supreme, when speaking of God, is above and beyond without any limits. No one else can come along later and become supreme. We don't like such terms because our finite minds are not able to fully comprehend. We can understand someone in first place. It just means he is a little better than the rest of the field. There is only room for one Supreme Being. Complete supremacy cannot be shared. If man were supreme in only one area, then God would lose His complete power.

Man sinned in the Garden and became separated from God. If it had been possible for man to have saved himself by a plan of his own, then God would not be supreme. The scheme of redemption required a Supreme Being. Because He is supreme Paul would declare:

*"All things are of God, who has reconciled
us to Himself through Jesus Christ, and
has given us the ministry of reconciliation."
(II Cor 5:18)*

*"One God and Father of all, who is
above all, and through all, and in you
all." (Eph 4:6)*

This is why worship that is designed to please men is vain. It does not allow God to be supreme. This is why every area of our life must come under His rule. This is why I can't say, "Lord, twenty-three hours of the day are yours. But I have reserved one hour each day for me." It just won't work.

Luke recorded a lesson Jesus taught so plainly one day on the road to Jerusalem. A man came up to Him and offered to follow Him. Jesus told Him that *"foxes have holes and birds have nest but He did not have a place to lay His head."* Luke doesn't tell us the man's response but it seems he was not that interested. Another man requested that he be allowed to return and bury his father. Jesus told him to *"let the dead bury their own dead."* Another man said he would follow but he just wanted to go and tell the people in his house good by. Jesus answer to this man had puzzled me for a long time. He said:

"No one having put his hand to the plow, and looking back, is fit for the kingdom of God."
(Lk 9:57-62)

This Scripture used to run through my mind

when I would be plowing on my father's farm. I have come to believe Jesus was simply trying to get these people (and us) to understand that following Him was an all or nothing proposition. God is supreme; nothing small or great can get in the way. This is why when the young man was told to sell all that he had and he refused, Jesus would not change the conditions just to please him.

Jesus said, *"I am the way the truth and the life."* If there was any other way, any other truth or any other life apart from Jesus He would not be the supreme God. This God's supremacy is a fundamental truth that cannot be compromised.

This is why alternatives are not to be considered. I had one man say to me one time, "Jesus made special provisions for the thief on the cross and I think He will make special provisions for me." But when Jesus was here as a man and was in such agony, He prayed, *"Father if it is Your will, remove this cup from Me; nevertheless not My will, but Yours be done."* In His humanity, He was submitting to the supremacy of the Father. We, too, can tell this God what we want, but the end must be "nevertheless" not my will but your supreme will be done.

This is why it is such an insult when men would

77

try to put anyone or anything equal with God. Some would say there are many gods and one is as good as another as long as you believe in a god. They tell us the only important thing is to believe in something. If this God is supreme, then such thinking is an insult to His character. This in essence would be idolatry.

Through out history we read of men who became very powerful but were corrupted. When they were found out, they went down in shame and disgrace. Now days we are reluctant to investigate our officials for fear of what we might find out they are doing behind our back; but this God, who is supreme to the infinite degree, has laid Himself open for full inspection. Since the Garden of Eden, mankind has been offering all kinds of excuses for his failures. He might even want to say it was impossible to live up to God's expectations, but He has forever removed that excuse. He disrobed Himself taking the form of man, and showed us with all His power and supremacy He is touchable. In all of His purity, He would touch the leper and allow the woman with the issue of blood to touch the helm of His garment. He is approachable. He is willing to become one of us. He is willing to endure the same temptations. He demonstrates that there is a better way to live. Finally, He would show us that though man might lay down his life for a friend in severe circumstances; this God would lay down His life for us while we were enemies. And being supreme He didn't have to do it. I fear we don't understand and appreciate the deliberate decision this supreme God made when He decided to sacrifice himself for us when He did not have to. We hear men say, "God sent His Son and they killed Him." That's true; but that's not the whole story. He willingly allowed them to kill Him. If they could have killed Him without His permission, He would not be supreme. This was a completely willing sacrifice.

Supreme means there can be no equal. There is only room for one supreme. To talk about another is a contradiction. Our faith is not just in some kind of a super being but the One and only supreme God. There is good reason the beloved apostle would say to those children of God.

> *"You are of God, little children, and have overcome them, because He who is in you is greater than he who is in the world." (I Jn 4:4)*

In the Garden of Eden the issue was the same. Adam and Eve wanted to have a vote in deciding what fruit to eat and not eat, and the war still goes on. When will man learn his best option is surrender?

So, don't shy away because He is so great. Draw close and allow Him to put His everlasting arms of love around you. He wants only your good. He wants you to love Him with all of your being. Remember that He has already loved you with all of His being first.

And, **THAT'S GOOD NEWS!**

Chapter Eight

A GOD WHO HAS NO LIMITS

*"Before the mountains were brought forth,
or ever You had formed the earth and the world,
even from everlasting to everlasting,
You are God."
(Ps 90:2)*

*"Now to Him who is able to do exceedingly
abundantly above all that we ask or think,
according to the power that works in us, to Him be
glory in the church by Christ Jesus to all
generations, forever and ever. Amen."
(Eph 3:20-21)*

Even King Solomon seemed to be overwhelmed with the thought of a God without limits when he said:

"But will God really dwell on earth?
The heavens, even the highest heaven,
cannot contain you. How much less this
temple I have built!"
(1 Kings 8:27)

When building the temple he confessed the impossibility to place limits of any kind on such a great God, as he exclaimed:

"And the house which I build is great;
for great is our God above all gods.
But who is able to build him a house,
seeing heaven and the heaven of
heavens cannot contain him? Who am I
then, that I should build Him a house,
save only to burn sacrifices
before Him."
(II Ch 2:5-7)

The sweet singer of Israel said,:
"Great is our Lord and mighty in power;

82

His understanding has no limit."
(Ps 147:5)
God spoke through the prophet:

"Can anyone hide in secret places so
that I cannot see him? declares the
Lord. Do not I fill heaven and earth?
declares the Lord."
(Jer 23:24)

Modern man with his high powered telescopes has not been able to see an end to space, and this verse declares, God fills it all.

"Can you fathom the mysteries of God?
Can you probe the limits of the
Almighty? They are higher than the
heavens – what can you do? They are
deeper than the depths of the grave –
what can you know? Their measure is
longer than the earth and
wider than the sea."
(Job 11:7-9)

When Job answered his friends and mentioned some of God's marvelous works he ended by saying:

> *"And these are but the outer fringe of*
> *His works; how faint the whisper we*
> *hear of Him! Who then can understand*
> *the thunder of His power?"*
> *(Job 26:14)*

This description by the Psalmist sums it up very well.

> *" Where can I go from Your Spirit?*
> *Or where can I flee from*
> *Your presence?*
> *If I ascend into heaven, You are there;*
> *If I make my bed in hell, behold,*
> *You are there.*
> *If I take the wings of the morning,*
> *And dwell in the uttermost parts*
> *of the sea,*
> *Even there Your hand shall lead me,*
> *And Your right hand shall hold me.*
> *If I say, "Surely the darkness*
> *shall fall on me,"*
> *Even the night shall be light about me;*
> *Indeed, the darkness shall not*
> *hide from You,*
> *But the night shines as the day;*

The darkness and the light are both
alike to You."
(Psa 137:7-12)

Through Isaiah, He shouts:

"For My thoughts are not your
thoughts, neither are your ways My
ways, says Jehovah. For as the heavens
are higher than the earth, so are My
ways higher than your ways, and My
thoughts than your thoughts."
(Isa 55:8-9 ASV)

The problem today is not the petty things which the church has spent its time discussing, arguing, and sometimes dividing over. Yes, these things are ugly, hateful, and a disgrace. Sadder yet, is that the glory of the Lord has departed. When Isaiah went to the temple what did he see? Chapter six says:

" I saw the Lord sitting on a throne,
high and lifted up, and the train of His
robe filled the temple. Above it stood
seraphim; each one had six wings: with

85

two he covered his face, with two he
covered his feet, and with two he flew."
(Isa 6:1-2)

Today people go to the house of worship, sit through service after service. They see the color of the tie the preacher wears; they see the actions of someone on the other side of the auditorium; they will comment about whether there were two or three songs; they note whether the sermon was fifteen or twenty minutes long; some will even notice if the pulpit has been moved a few inches, but in all their life have they ever seen the glory of the Lord? Yes, I know, some are more interested in being entertained. One little boy remarked on the way home, "I think it was a pretty good show. We all got in for a dollar."

I fear many who may have seen what they thought was God may turn out to be very different from the God the writers of the Bible knew. This god we have made, and because we have made him we can understand him. Man wants a god he thinks he understands and to some degree at least control.

"O the depth of the riches both of the

wisdom and the knowledge of God!
How unsearchable are His judgments
and His ways past tracing out!"
(Rom 11:33 ASV)

Wycliffe Bible Commentary offers these comments on Romans 11:33-36:

> *"Depth – God's riches, wisdom and knowledge are inexhaustible. His decisions or decrees are beyond man's capacity to fathom. His ways – the whole of his conduct – cannot be followed through and tracked out. No man is great enough to observe all of God's actions and to follow them through."*

The OT quotations (Isa 40:13; Job 41:11) show God's independence from man. Finally, in one mighty surge of devotion, Paul attributes glory to God forever, the God who is the Source, Sustainer, and Goal of all things.

And Paul humbly acknowledges his position as a servant:

"Unto me, who am less than the least of

*all the saints, this grace was given, that
I should preach among the Gentiles the
unsearchable riches of Christ."*
(Eph 3:8)

Hear the words of Anselm:

*"Up now, slight man! Flee for a little
while thy occupations; hide thyself for a
time from thy disturbing thoughts. Cast
aside now thy burdensome cares, and
put away thy toilsome business. Yield
room for some little time to God, and
rest for a little time in Him. Enter the
inner chamber of thy mind; shut out all
thoughts save that of God and such as
can aid thee in seeking Him. Speak
now, my whole heart! Speak now to
God, saying, I seek Thy face; Thy face,
Lord, will I seek."*
(St. Anselm, op.cit.P.3.)

Of all that can be thought about or said about
God, His limitlessness (or infinite) is among the
most difficult for us to grasp. To even try almost
seems contradictory because it requires knowing

before hand we can never fully comprehend it. Yet something in us yearns to know. In His Holy revelation, He tells us He is infinite and along with His other attributes we must accept this one too.

We need not be discouraged and turn back because the climb is difficult and because we will never reach the top. Like the mountain climber, the higher we climb the greater will be the view. The more we see Him as He is; the more we will love Him. The more we love Him; the more we will want to serve Him. The more we serve Him; the more we will become like Him. The more we become like Him; the more we will have fulfilled our purpose for living. You can almost see the great apostle Paul as he is trying to find the words to express what he wants to say:

"O the depths of the riches both of the wisdom and knowledge of God! How unsearchable are His judgments, and His ways past finding out!"
(Rom 11:33)

In this effort to better understand who this God really is, we are trying to understand a being altogether foreign to us. And, like the Israelites at

89

Mt. Sinai, we can only come so close and no farther. It is unlike anything we can relate to in our world of matter, space and time. In this, we pass beyond our power of conception. Because He is greater than the human mind, the mind can never completely conceive Him. Were we able to conceive of His greatness, He would be less than the human mind and that would be a god too small. He is greater than all language, so no words can adequately express Him. If it could, He would be less than human speech. All our thoughts and words will fall short of fully expressing what He is. But we are only required to accept that which He has graciously revealed for our finite minds. He made us, therefore He knows how much we need and can understand. For the remainder, we just trust.

A word of warning here. We need to be careful in the use of terms that can apply to God alone. If we use them too lightly, they tend to lose some of their real meaning and, in turn, some of His true glory is marred.

In our modern culture, the word infinite has not always been held to its precise meaning. When we say the craftsman takes infinite pains to make sure his work is the best or the gardener takes infinite care with the flowers we simply mean much or a great deal. This word along with certain others should only be used of this one God. There is no other truly infinite being.

When we say that God is infinite, we mean He knows no bounds. Whatever He is, and all He is, He is without limit. Again, we speak of unlimited wealth, and boundless energy. But there is no unlimited wealth or boundless energy, unless we are speaking of the wealth and energy of God.

When we say God is infinite, we say He is measureless. We measure thing as a way we have of accounting for these things for ourselves. It describes limits, imperfections which can never be applied to God. We try to measure abstract qualities; we speak of great or little faith, high or low intelligence, large or meager talents. These are good for measuring the things we work with that He has created, but should never be used the way we see Him. He is above all this, outside of it, beyond it.

All that He is He is without limits. Degrees do not apply. Nothing in God is less or more, large or small. He is what He is in Himself without qualifying thought or word. He is simply God. There are untold hidden things in the natural world and certainly the Spiritual that are reserved for Him alone, and we need not concern ourselves with them. Let us just let Him be God. Paul assured the Ephesians their trust in God is not misguided:

> *"...that their hearts may be encouraged, being knit together in love, and attaining to all riches of the full assurance of understanding, to the knowledge of the mystery of God, both of the Father and of Christ, in whom are hidden all the treasures of wisdom and knowledge."*
> *(Col 2:2-3)*

His Word warns us not to add to or take away from His revelation and surely this applies to what He has revealed about Himself. To think such would be presumption. It is enough to know that God is God.

Because God is infinite, everything that flows out of His nature is infinite also. We become frustrated with all the limitations imposed upon us as human beings. *"The days and years of our lives are few, and swifter than a weaver's shuttle."* Someone has described it thus: *"Life is a short and fevered rehearsal for a concert we cannot stay to give. Just when we seem to have gained some proficiency we are forced to lay our instruments down. There is simply not enough time to think, to become, to practice and perform all that the constitution of our nature indicates we are capable of." (Unknown)*

Have you ever wondered why the more you study His Word, the more you realize you need to study? The more you understand, the more you realize you don't understand? Each time you learn the answer to one question, new questions arise?

It is comforting in the face of all our limitations to turn to God who has none. Eternal years lie in His heart. For Him time does not pass, it remains; and if we are in Him we share with Him and He has no problem giving us eternal life. He never hurries. No wonder the Word declares;

"For a thousand years in Your sight are
like yesterday when it is past, are like
a watch in the night." (Ps 90:4-5)

There is no deadline against which He must work. This should help calm our spirits and relax our nerves. The words of an old song says, *"Fear not, I am with thee. O be not dismayed, for I am thy God and will still give thee aid."*

God's handiwork in nature is limited. These things are finite because they are created. The time will come when *"He will roll them up as a vesper."* But the free gift of eternal life He has promised us in Christ Jesus is as limitless as God Himself. God gives of that which is Himself. There is eternal life enough in God for everyone, and, He has no difficulty with giving eternal life to everyone who will come to Him. This is why Jesus could say and John could confidently write:

"And this is eternal life, that they may know you, the only one true God, and Jesus Christ whom You have sent."
(Jn 17:3)

This is why Paul could write: *"Where sin abounded, grace did much more abound."* Abounding sin is the terror of the world, but the more abounding grace of this God is the hope of mankind. However sin may abound it has limits, for is the product of man's finite minds and stubborn will; but God's "much more" tells us He is infinite in character.

Every essential doctrine of the Christian faith is supported by the unlimited nature of our God.

94

Some have questioned the eternal nature of hell, but the limitless character of both heaven and hell are true because they are in perfect keeping with the nature of God Himself.

This is why the Christian's hope is not based on our own abilities which are so limited, but on the unlimited ability of this God. This is why the sacrifice He made can not be limited to only a few sins, but is sufficient to cover all the sins that will ever be committed. This is why no matter how deep into sin you may have fallen; you are not beyond the reach of His forgiveness. The Hebrew writer concerning the Christ could declare:

"He is able to save to the UTTERMOST
all who come to God through Him."
(Heb 7:25)

This is why Paul could write with such confidence:

"Nothing will ever be able to separate
us from the love of God in
Christ Jesus our Lord."
(Rom 8:39)

The mercy of God is infinite also, and all who have felt the pain of guilt know this is more than academic.

Even that golden text of the Bible would lose its significance without the limitless nature of God. If there were any limit to Him, there might be one soul so lost in sin who His love could not reach. That's why the gospel is such good news to all sinners. Preachers and all who would proclaim it need not be afraid to tell all sinners: God is willing and able to save. One song says, *"Tell to sinners far and wide, Jesus saves."*

Joseph Hart wrote:

> *"This is the God we adore, Our faithful un-changeable Friend, Whose love is as great as His power, and neither knows no measure nor end.*
> *This Jesus the first and the last, Whose Spirit shall guide us safe home; We'll praise Him for all that is past, and trust Him for all that's to come."*

Walter A. Ogden wrote the old song that says:

96

Tis the grandest theme
through the ages rung;
Tis the grandest theme
for a mortal tongue;
Tis the grandest theme
that the world e'er sung.
Our God is able to deliver thee.

And, **THAT'S GOOD NEWS!**

Chapter Nine

IMMUTABLE

"Wherein God, willing more abundantly to show unto the heirs of promise the immutability of His counsel, confirmed it with an oath: That by two immutable things in which it was impossible for God to lie, we might have a strong consolation, who have fled for refuge to lay hold on the hope that is set before us."

(Heb 6:17-18)

The definition for the term *Immutable* is: unchangeable. When an object is defined as being immutable, it means it is not subject or susceptible to change.

One thing wrong with these definitions is God cannot be initialized because He is immutable from all eternity; He needs no initializing. So in using this term, as well as many others, we need to understand we cannot hold this God up to our human scrutiny. Perhaps the one advantage is we don't hear the term immutable used very much in the public arena. This is good because it seems the more we use terms the more they lose their original meaning.

We all learned the story of the little boy who could not tell a lie. He cut down the cherry tree and when asked if he did it he answered, "I cannot tell a lie. I did it." Some have argued the story itself is not so because as humans we all know it is possible for us to lie. We may not always lie when asked about something, but we do choose to lie or tell the truth.

Again, left to our own reasoning we would think God Himself would be able to choose whether to tell the truth or lie. This God has not left us to just imagine what He is like. Knowing all about us thought we needed to be assured of His Immutable nature. God does not just decide to tell the truth; He cannot do otherwise. This is why in the opening Scripture for this chapter we are told *"He swore by Himself."*

Immutability is the attribute that undergirds every action of God and allows us to trust completely in the promises and actions of this God. We really don't have as much difficulty understanding this attribute. Our greatest need here is the same as with other attributes. It starts with humbly acknowledging this God is God and we are not. It's not about us. It's all about Him.

Until we bring our basic thinking into line with the way God has revealed Himself, the conflict will continue. We cannot think the same about this God as when we think of created human beings. I saw a bumper sticker which said; God said it, I believe it and that settles it." It really should say: "God said it; that settles it and I need to believe it."

When we say God is immutable, when God says He is immutable, He is saying He can be trusted. Yes, He has said the same thing in a lot of different ways but sometimes things are said in different ways to emphasis its importance. All through the Old Testament God was pleading with His chosen people; "Trust Me." To be completely trusted He must be immutable; not subject to change. The idea that God started out one way and as time progressed the need for change arose and God has changed is close to being blasphemous and should never enter our minds.

One thing is certain, we mortal beings can and do change. Any one who has not changed has not lived very long. When we change it will be in possibly three different directions. Our actions may be from good to bad or from bad to good. Or our thinking or belief may change. No such changes can ever be expected from God. He has always been perfect therefore He can not change for the better. And God forbid we should even think He would change for the worse. Thank God we as humans can change and thank God He can't.

When we consider His other attributes, His self-sufficiency, His eternal nature, His all knowing, all wise nature, it is easy to see He must be immutable.

Most Bible believers agree that His Word is unchangeable and has been once and for all revealed. We need not expect another revelation that will modify any part. This in spite of the fact that some today think because our world is so different from the world when it was written that we need an updated version. That Word is immutable because this God who has spoken is immutable. He will not become dissatisfied with the writers and choose replacements to edit and update it. This is how we know those today who claim to have some special revelation are false when their revelation is different. This is the test for all teachers and preachers when you claim to be speaking for God. You need to make sure your message agrees with what He has already said.

As in the other attributes we ask, of what use to me is all this? In this world men forget us and change their attitude toward us as their interest dictates. To know a God that is immutable is a source of strength. When Jesus was here in the flesh, the one thing the Jewish people refused to admit was His claim to be God. Some of Jesus' statements angered them to the point of wanting to kill Him. They knew too well if these statements were true then He must be God. On one occasion He said, *"I am the way the truth and the life."* Notice He did not just say I tell the truth, but *"I am the truth."* When He tells the truth, He is not upholding some standard of truth. He is the standard and truth itself is judged by Him. When we come to Him in prayer, we need not worry whether we will find Him in a receptive mood. He does not keep office hours or set aside times when He will see no one. His love for us will never change. Today He feels the same about us as He did the day He let Jesus die for us. We can also know that His attitude toward sin is the same it was when He drove Adam from the Garden of Eden. We believe what He says in His Word not because the Bible is a nice book. It is impossible for it to be wrong. It is not just true beyond reasonable doubt. It is not that God has never told a lie, but it is impossible for Him to ever tell a lie.

I believe greatly in prayer. I believe my prayers have been heard and answered always in good ways, but not always in the way I wanted. His answer is always good. However, I don't believe my prayers ever changed God. I am all for efforts to get God's people to pray more. At the same time, we need to understand millions of people praying will never be successful in getting God to do something against His nature. Anytime we are talking about change it must take place from our end, we can change, He can't.

God cannot be coaxed into a compromise. He cannot be persuaded to alter His word nor talked into answering selfish prayers. That is why, in all our efforts to find God, to please Him, to commune with Him, all change must take place on our part.

"I am the Lord, I change not."
(Mal 3:6)

The Hebrew writer, showing that Jesus is God, declared:

"Thy throne, O God, is forever and ever... And You,, Lord, in the beginning laid the foundation of the earth; and the heavens are the works of Your hands; They will perish, but You remain; And they will all grow old like a garment; like a cloak You will fold them up, and they will be changed. But You are the same, and Your years will not fail."
(quotes from Heb 1)

What is needed is very clear. We must hear His clearly stated terms, and bring our lives into accord with His revealed will. All the force of His immutability stands behind every promise that He has made. Our hope in Him is both sure and steadfast and is the anchor of the soul.

Because this God is immutable, sinner beware! God cannot be toyed with. He hates sin and has said unless you repent, you will perish. No popular vote can change that. Objectors marching in the streets will not persuade Him to grant unreasonable demands. His offer of mercy and salvation by grace to all is still good. It cannot be countermanded because He is immutable. He says, you have My word, *"Whoever comes to me I will in no wise cast out."* Don't you want to serve a God like that?

Taking this God seriously is not just a good policy for our culture to follow. It's a matter of life and death. It's not just something that would make this world a better place to live, but these are eternal matters.

All this is why this God is not a "take it or leave it proposition." This is why He cannot accept half-hearted, lukewarm, indifferent commitment; it makes Him sick. This is why He says *"He that is not with Me is against Me."* And if you are with Him, He promises *"I will never leave you nor forsake you."* David was not just a wild eyed dreamer when he wrote: *"Thy rod and thy staff they comfort me."* That assurance is promised to whosoever will come to Him. From One who is *Immutable*, that's a good deal. The one who turns it down is a fool.

And, **That's Good News!**

Chapter Ten

ALMIGHTY

"And I heard, as it were, the voice of a great multitude, as the sound of many waters and as the sound of mighty thundering, saying, "Alleluia! For the Lord God Omnipotent reigns! Let us be glad and rejoice."
(Rev 19:67)

"But I saw no temple in it, for the Lord God Almighty and the Lamb are its temple."
(Rev 21:22)

I am afraid we finite beings read such statements, but do not allow the deep truth to sink in. We skip over and go on to what we consider more pleasant things to think about. To think on the character of this God requires serious thought, and we seem to prefer the lighter side. In fact, I have had people remark "you take things too seriously." Humans have tried to explain this God in what would be more acceptable terms that would not require either time or thought, but this God is too big for that.

The Latin word *Omnipotence* is the word translated many times to speak of God being all powerful. Its meaning is the same as the more familiar *Almighty* which comes from the Anglo-Saxon. The word is found some fifty-six times in the Bible. It is another of those terms that is never used of anyone but God. This is the word we have chosen to use more in this chapter. It is a word that men have misused at times. We hear people say such things as "the almighty dollar." It's true the dollar wields a lot of power in our world, but it is far from almighty. We see in our world around us the power of God at work, and we depend on it everyday. He keeps the worlds in their proper orbit, and there is never a collision. We don't go to bed at night afraid we will wakeup in the morning and our planet will be somewhere on the other side of Mars. The God in charge of this universe is powerful. He is dependable as well because He is all powerful. This alone is enough that Paul would declare to the Romans in chapter one that man is without excuse in knowing He exists and is powerful. This is enough to cause rational thinking individuals to give serious consideration to what He has to say.

We have seen the things men have made and conclude that man does have considerable power. But man's power is limited to working with the things God has created. Man has no power at all to create anything beyond that which already exists. Thus the power we see in man can never be compared to the power of this God.

Any power we as finite beings have has been delegated to us. All the things in nature, the sun, moon and stars all do their perfect work to bring glory to God. So, when man uses the limited powers delegated to him in a proper way, he brings glory to his Creator as well. It is notable that some of the most powerful people in history who have done some of the greatest things give all the credit to the Creator and admit that they are only vessels through which He works.

Ours is a God who speaks and worlds come into existence from nothing. A God who speaks and dead men come back to life requires almighty power. There must never be the possibility of another power that could stand in the way of His purpose.

Everything about this God is infinite (without limits). Therefore, He is infinite in power as well. *"Power belonged unto God,"* said the Psalmist. He was saying all power not just some power. Paul declared to the Romans in chapter one that nature itself gives evidence of the eternal power of this God. From this knowledge, it is easy to reason that He is omnipotent. This power was not given to Him from another source. He is the source of all the power, and since the source must be equal to anything that emanates from it, God is equal to all the power there is. This is another way to say, "He is Almighty."

As a person reads the Scriptures they will readily see there is a radical difference in the way modern man and the men of the Bible looks at this world. Where the men of the Bible saw God, modern man sees the laws of nature. Some even think that given time he will figure out a way to even control it also.

The trustworthiness of God's behavior in His world is the foundation of all scientific truth. The scientist puts his faith in those laws even though he may not admit they are God's laws. From there, he goes on to achieve many useful things in a number of areas. The believer on the other hand, puts his faith in God behind all nature. Believers are more concerned with the One who made it all.

In the famous "Monkey Trial" conducted in Dayton, Tennessee, the teaching of evolution in the public schools was being tried. Williams Jennings Bryan was on the witness stand and was being questioned by the famous Clarence Darrow. Darrow framed his question very carefully. "Scientist tells us the earth is millions of years old and your religion says the earth is only six thousand years old; how do you answer that?" Bryan answered, *I would rather trust in the rock of ages than to know the age of the rocks.* Mr. Darrow did not like the answer but he did not choose to challenge it.

IN THE BEGINNING

It is surely no accident that the Bible begins with

111

the statement "In the beginning God...." Everything begins with Him who really has no beginning. The complete book of Genesis is a revelation of the power of God at work in the creation and setting in order all things in this universe. This is no accident. God did not start somewhere in the middle. He started at the beginning and the beginning is God. He is a God that is all powerful and because He is the all powerful creator, who made everything from nothing, man can only refuse to listen to Him at his own peril. If there is any lesson we should learn, it is this. God is the ruler of this universe. He made it. He sustains it. It answers to Him and Him alone. He is the Creator; we are the created; and the created has no right to question the one who made it, *"Why did you make me this way?"* Once this question is settled, all future questions will be easy to answer. My suggestion to anyone who reads the first few chapters of Genesis, STOP! Make sure you are in agreement with this God that He is God. He is the Creator. He is the all powerful God. So, He has the sovereign right to rule my life as well. Until this question is settled, little will be gained by continuing to read. It will probably do like my father used to say to me, *"Is what I'm saying just going in one ear and out the other?"* Yes, we will read it. But after we have read it, we will go on and live our lives the same old way.

For a promise to have meaning, the one who makes the promise must have the power to fulfill that promise and the will to carry through. If either is lacking, the promise cannot be depended on. The God of the Bible has made some incredible promises. Unless He has all power, there might be someone or something that could keep Him from fulfilling His promise. The surety of our faith is dependent upon God's ability to keep His promise. We don't understand how He will do it; when He will do it. There are a number of things we don't understand, but this much we know for sure; He is able and willing.

Some special verses come to mind that say it so well.

"And God is able to make all grace abound toward you, that you, always having all sufficiency in all things, may have abundance for every good work. As it is written: He has dispersed abroad, He has given to the poor; His righteousness endures forever.'"
(II Co 9:8-10)

113

"Now to Him who is able to do exceedingly abundantly above all that we ask or think, according to the power that works in us…"
(Eph 3:20-21)

With God having all power, not only can He do anything He chooses to do; one thing is as easy for Him as another, He is not dependent on the assistance of weak human beings but is able to do everything that is good that needs to be done. No wonder Paul could write:

"I know in whom I have believed and am persuaded that He is able to keep that which I have committed to Him until that day."
(II Tim 2:12b)

And he could continue:
"And we know that all things work together for good to those who love God, to those who are the called according to His purpose.
(Rom 8:28)

The power of God is not just academic. It is relevant to our everyday walk. We find great comfort in a relationship with the One who possesses all power; especially when we are confident that power will work for us and not against us. "If God be for us, who can be against us." Amen

God is not like a battery that runs down and has to be recharged. When the going gets tough, these words from Isaiah help to keep me going:

> *"Have you not known? Have you not heard? The everlasting God, the Lord, the Creator of the ends of the earth, neither faints nor is weary. His understanding is unsearchable. He gives power to the weak, And to those who have no might, He increases strength. Even the youths shall faint and be weary, And the young men shall utterly fall, But those who wait on the Lord shall renew their strength; They shall mount up with wings like eagles, They shall run and not be weary, They shall walk and not faint."*
> *(Isa 40:28-31)*

And, **THAT'S GOOD NEWS!**

Chapter Eleven

HE IS SOVEREIGN

"'Stand up, son of man,' said the Voice. 'I want to speak with you.' The Spirit came into me as He spoke and set me on my feet. I listened carefully to his words. 'Son of man,' He said, 'I am sending you to the nation of Israel, a nation that is rebelling against me. Their ancestors have rebelled against me from the beginning, and they are still in revolt to this very day. They are a hard-hearted and stubborn people. But I am sending you to say to them, **'This is what the Sovereign LORD says!'** *And whether they listen or not — for remember, they are rebels at least they will know they have had a prophet among them.'"*
(Ezk 2:1-5)NLT

I am convinced that man with his pride has the greatest difficulty dealing with the sovereignty of God. When we speak of sovereignty, we are thinking about authority. To be sovereign, not only must God have all authority, He must be completely free. There can be nothing to stand in His way. Man has great difficulty admitting that he does not have the final word.

We live in a country where we have individual freedom to believe and practice whatever we choose. Somehow we conclude that whatever we chose is right, and no one (not even God) should dare question our choice. We hear these statements: "what is right for you may not be right for me; each person has to make the decision for themselves; no one should try to judge another person concerning what is right or what is wrong." All this is the result of man thinking his own understanding is the highest authority there is. An acceptance of the sovereignty of God and application to everyday life will turn much of this modern thinking upside down. Another problem man has to deal with is the idea that whatever the majority thinks should be the rule. Modern man feels the pull of such forces, and he is faced with the decision on what or who will set the standard for how he lives.

Adam and Eve were faced with this basic decision in the beginning when God gave them their first instruction concerning what they were to eat. Instead of accepting God's instruction as final and best, they decided they should also take into consideration what the Serpent had to say (It's always good to get a second opinion). Their final decision was that the Serpent knew better than God. After they had listened to the Serpent and analyzed the situation, their conclusion was that there was no good reason not to eat of the forbidden fruit. Needless to say, you and I today live in a world that reeks with the consequences of that decision.

God Declares His Sovereignty

God's first commandment given through Moses was, *"Thou shall have no other gods before Me." (Ex 20:3)* It surely is no accident this is the first commandment. This concept must be firmly fixed in our hearts, or we will have difficulty with every other commandment. When God told Moses to go back to Egypt and deliver His people, Moses was concerned about whether the Israelites people would accept him as the one to deliver them from Egyptian bondage. So, God told him to tell the people *"I AM HAS SENT ME UNTO YOU." (Ex 3:14b)* This was a way of saying, "I come by the authority of the highest authority there is."

When Moses told Pharaoh this God said for him to let His people go, Pharaoh had the same problem not accepting the sovereignty of God. However, when God was finished with that tenth plague, Pharaoh had no difficulty understanding that God was sovereign.

God Repeats Some Things Over And Over

Someone with authority should not have to repeat something over and over. Surely with all authority, it is not necessary for God to repeat Himself, but some things He has repeated many times. If I have counted correctly, God is referred to as "The Sovereign Lord" in the book of Ezekiel over two hundred times (NLT). In the book of Amos, sixteen times He is referred to as "the Sovereign Lord." The Bible truly is a book about the Sovereign Lord.

Jesus said:

> *"All authority has been given to Me in heaven and on earth. Go therefore and make disciples of all the nations, baptizing them in the name of the Father and of the Son and of the Holy Spirit, teaching them to observe all things that I have commanded you; and lo, I am with you always, even to the end of the age. Amen."*
> *(Matt 28:18-20)*

Notice Jesus says this authority has been bestowed on Him, and He commands by the authority of the total Godhead. This shows what we have said before: "All of God does all that God does." When these apostles taught, when they baptized, and when they taught the things He had commanded them, it had all the authority of the sovereign Godhead's approval. I fear we fail to realize what it really means when we say "The Word of God is inspired." There is a sovereign God that stands backing up every word.

I realize we are living in a society that wants to be so inclusive that it is not politically correct to say there is only one God. This is offensive to not only those who believe there are other gods. Some claim to believe in one God but just keep their belief to themselves lest they rock the boat. It may be hard to believe, but there are churches that teach those who even deny the existence of God should be included. If they are sincere, no one should question whether they are right or wrong.

This God is sovereign because He is the "all powerful" God. If there was anything He did not have power over, He would not be sovereign; His rule would break down at that point. He is sovereign because He is the "all knowing" God. If any knowledge existed outside of Him, He would not be sovereign. To rule over all, He must be sovereign. He must be completely free to act without any outside force to interfere. We talk about being free as a bird but a bird is a long way from being completely free.

This God revealed in the Holy Scriptures does not require permission from anyone or anything. *Who is higher than the highest? Who is mightier that the Almighty? Who can question one of His decisions? Who can countermand even one of His orders?* NO ONE!

In face of the well established truth about His sovereignty, some seem to think they can question His actions. For example, they ask. "If God is sovereign, how can He allow so much evil to exist? Why does He allow human suffering? Why does He allow an innocent child to suffer and die so young and a wicked person to live to a ripe old age? All these questions seem to cry out for an answer. Believers admit they do not have the answer; especially an answer that will satisfy man who feels he is self-sufficient. When we ask these questions, we know our answers are not sufficient. We don't possess all wisdom. We don't have the answers. We are not in control. Our sin is not that we have questions; rather, we don't seem to be willing to accept the answer. When the sovereign God refuses to answer our questions to our satisfaction, we rebel. It's as if He is somehow under obligation to not only answer but to answer the way we want. Remember, if He had to answer every question the finite mind of man could come up with, He would not be sovereign. He would not be God.

I watched a man on TV recently who went through a long list of accusations "If God did this and if God did that it would be such a terrible thing." On and on he went. As I listened I could not help but think; this man seems to think he has the right to put God on the witness stand and cross-examine everything He has ever said or done. This man did know some verses of Scripture, but he did not accept the sovereignty of God. If God is Sovereign, then Paul would declare:

"Certainly not! Indeed, let God be true

but every man a liar. As it is written:
'That You may be justified in Your words,
and may overcome when You are judged.'"
(Rom 3:4)

Friend, Paul was saying, if you argue with God He will win, so don't try it.

I can well remember when I was growing up my father would tell us to do something, and I did not understand his reasoning. Sometimes I would question, and the answer I got did not please me. Looking back I realize now he knew what he was doing, but he had difficulty explaining it to me in terms I could understand because I was a child. I think I did understand that his answer was final, and my best course was to accept it and go on. But sometimes my stubborn will would get in the way. He wanted to teach me there are times when I don't have the right to question. I have heard preachers say, "It's alright to question God." I believe that is terrible advice to give anyone. Stubborn man must learn submission and submission begins with admitting that God is sovereign.

Sometimes we hear the question, "If God

has all power and is sovereign, then why does He not stop some evil from happening or why does He not stop the terrible disease of cancer in its track once and for all?" I don't claim to know why He does some of the things He does. But this I do know. To have all power and to be sovereign, He does not have to do everything He could do. As a sovereign God, He has the right to choose to do or not to do and being sovereign there is no one in position to question His decision. That is what it means to be sovereign. If God was ever wrong (which He could never be), no one would be smart enough to know it. And if anyone was smart enough to know it (which is not possible), they still would not have the right to question. Our problem is we have difficulty accepting what it means to be sovereign to the infinite degree.

Some question how God can be sovereign and man can still have free will. Our finite minds have such difficulty even trying to think in terms of the infinite (that which is without limits). This is where we must walk by faith and not by sight. However, this should give us great comfort to know the

One in control is sovereign. This enables us to sleep well at night. No power can interfere with Him. This gives us courage to walk during the day. "I *can do all things through Christ who strengthens me.*" "*He is my shepherd, I shall be well supplied.*" And yes, "*Even though I walk through that dark valley called death, I will fear no evil.*" Why? Because a sovereign God who is infinite in wisdom and power loves me with a love that surpasses understanding. He will never leave me nor forsake me. He will not allow me to be tempted beyond what I am able to bear but will always provide a way of escape. "*I am persuaded that He is able (and He is sovereign) to keep that which I have committed to Him against that day.*"

It should not be that hard to live by faith in such a God. We should be able to sing:

I care not today what tomorrow my bring,
If shadow or sunshine or rain,
The Lord I know ruleth o'er everything,
And all of my worry is vain.
Living by faith, In Jesus above,
Trusting confiding in His great love;

From all harm safe, In His sheltering arm,
I'm living by faith and feel no alarm.
(words by James Wells)

OUR GOD IS AN AWESOME SOVEREIGN GOD!

And, **THAT'S GOOD NEWS!**

Chapter Twelve

HOLY

"Because I know that the Spirit of the
Holy God *is in you."*
the words of Nebuchadnezzer to Daniel
(Dan 4:9a)

Because it is written,
"Be holy, for I am holy."
(I Pet 1:16)

If anything has been lacking in this generation, it has been an emphasis on the holiness of God. As a result, I have noticed a much too casual approach to God. When one young man was asked to lead a prayer on Sunday morning, he began, "Hi, God." Far be it from me to judge the heart of this young man, but this just seems more like the way you would greet a casual friend you met on the street. Surely when we approach God, we are not equals. There's a song that says, *"My God and I go through the fields together, we walk and talk as good friends should and do."* It's true that if I am His child we are friends, but this is not a buddy-buddy relationship. We walk together, but we are not on equal footing. He is the Father; I am the child. He is Lord; I am His subject. He is Master; I am His slave.

If there is one chapter where the holiness of God stands out and should get our attention, I believe it is Exodus chapter nineteen. This is where God was preparing the people for the giving of the Ten Commandments and other instructions that would serve as the guiding principles for His people throughout their generations. I call this the "Preamble" to the Ten Commandments. Before God would speak and write these commandments on tablets of stone, these people needed to understand just who He is and how holy He is. Otherwise there was the danger of taking what He was going to say too lightly. I am convinced the same need exist today. Unless we understand how holy the One is who is speaking to us, we may read His Word in the same casual way we would the daily newspaper or the Readers Digest. Following is the instruction God gave before He wrote the Ten Commandments on the stone tablets:

Exodus Chapter Nineteen:

"In the third month after the children of Israel were gone forth out of the land of Egypt, the same day came they into the wilderness of Sinai.

And when they were departed from Rephidim, and were come to the wilderness of Sinai, they encamped in the wilderness; and there Israel encamped before the mount.

And Moses went up unto God, and Jehovah called unto him out of the mountain, saying, Thus shall thou say to the house of Jacob, and tell the children of Israel:

Ye have seen what I did unto the Egyptians, and how I bore you on eagles' wings, and brought you unto myself. Now therefore, if ye will obey my voice indeed, and keep my covenant, then ye shall be mine own possession from among all peoples: for all the earth is mine: and ye shall be unto me a kingdom of priests and a holy nation. These are the words which thou shall speak unto the children of Israel.

And Moses came and called for the elders of the people, and set before them all these words which Jehovah commanded him. And all the people answered together, and said, All that Jehovah hath spoken we will do. And Moses reported the words of the people unto Jehovah. And Jehovah said unto Moses, Lo, I come unto thee in a thick cloud, that the people may hear when I speak with thee, and may also believe thee for ever. And Moses told the words of the people unto Jehovah. And Jehovah said unto Moses, Go unto the people, and sanctify them today and tomorrow, and let them wash their garments, and be ready against the third day; for the third day Jehovah will come down in the sight of all the people upon Mount Sinai.

And thou shall set bounds unto the people round about, saying, Take heed to yourselves, that ye go not up into the mount, or touch the border of it: whosoever touches the mount shall be surely put to death: no hand shall touch him, but he shall surely be stoned, or shot through; whether it be beast or man, he shall not live: when the trumpet sounds long, they shall come up to the mount.

And Moses went down from the mount unto the people, and sanctified the people; and they washed their garments. And he said unto the people, be ready against the third day: come not near a woman. And it came to pass on the third day, when it was morning, that there were thunders and lightening, and a thick cloud upon the mount, and the voice of a trumpet exceeding loud; and all the people that were in the camp trembled.

And Moses brought forth the people out of the camp to meet God; and they stood at the nether part of the mount. And Mount Sinai, the whole of it, smoked, because Jehovah descended upon it in fire; and the smoke thereof ascended as the smoke of a furnace, and the whole mount quaked greatly.

And when the voice of the trumpet waxed louder and louder, Moses spoke, and God answered him by a voice. And Jehovah came down upon Mount Sinai, to the top of the mount: and Jehovah called Moses to the top of the mount; and Moses went up.

And Jehovah said unto Moses, Go down, charge the people, lest they break through unto Jehovah to

132

gaze, and many of them perish. And let the priests also, that come near to Jehovah, sanctify themselves, lest Jehovah break forth upon them.

And Moses said unto Jehovah, The people cannot come up to Mount Sinai: for thou didst charge us, saying, Set bounds about the mount, and sanctify it. And Jehovah said unto him, Go, get thee down; and thou shall come up, thou, and Aaron with thee: but let not the priests and the people break through to come up unto Jehovah, lest he break forth upon them. So Moses went down unto the people, and told them."

For a long time I confess I had read the Ten Commandments in chapter twenty but had passed over this chapter nineteen. When I did realize these things were a prelude, even the commandments take on a greater importance. I had the privilege of going down into the old Maritime Prison in Rome from where Paul wrote the second letter to Timothy. After seeing that place, I appreciate the words he wrote much more. In the same way, now before I read the Ten Commandments I like to read this chapter and then I listen more intently to the commandments. These are not just Ten Commandments that were arbitrarily chosen but they flow out of the very nature of God; they are based on His attribute of holiness.

When the sons of Aaron went about their priestly duties, they wore on their vest a plate made of pure gold with the words "HOLY TO JEHOVAH" engraved upon it. This was so they would always be reminded who they belonged to and who they were serving. When we read all the special instructions for the activities in the Tabernacle and later in the temple, each of them had special meaning because they were in the presence of the holy God and man was not free to do just anything and in any way he chose. We have only to read the story of Nadab and Abihu, the two sons of Aaron the high priest, who decided to take matters into their own hand recorded in Leviticus chapter ten. They learned the hard way that just anything did not go.

The book of Leviticus is filled with instructions concerning many actions which this holy God would not condone and the punishment for those who practiced such. Over and over God tells the people, you are to be a holy people; I am holy and as My people you must be holy.

I hear people saying today that we cannot live holy lives. God thought His people in the Old Testament could be holy and if they committed some of these things He said, they were to be put to death. It really was and is a matter of life and death. Just before they were to cross over into the Promised Land, Moses rehearses the Law with them and he says:

> *"I call heaven and earth as witnesses today against you, that I have set before you life and death, blessing and cursing; therefore choose life that both you and your descendants may live;*
> *(Duet 30:19)*

This is the sad state of affairs in our culture today. Many of the very things which God ordered people put to death for, because they were such an offence to His Holy nature, are considered just an alternate lifestyle. It is felt that no one has any right to question and really it's personal and should remain private.

We are not very shocked by some of these things today. It may be because we have rebelled against the will of this Holy God for so long. We no longer feel any guilt and we are left with a cancer of the soul; a disease called sin that is rotting away at our being and affecting even the environment in which we live.

In Isaiah chapter 6: Isaiah saw The Holy God *"high and lifted up."* The Seraphims above the throne cried out to each other, *"Holy, Holy. Holy is the Lord of host"* and when Isaiah saw this God, he painfully cried:

> *"Woe is me! For I am undone; because I am a man of unclean lips, and I dwell in the midst of a people of unclean lips: for mine eyes have seen the King, the Lord of hosts."* (Isa 6:5)

Isaiah was expressing a feeling that every man who truly comes to see this Holy God feels. Only when we see this Holy God as He is, will we see ourselves as we really are and, like Isaiah, be willing to take on the wicked conditions around us. But when we do, we may not be so comfortable with ourselves and like Isaiah cry *"Woe is me."*

We live in the midst of so much unholiness that it has become the normal and holiness the abnormal. We no longer expect honesty and faithfulness in those we deal with. When our politicians lie to us its no big deal. One lady said to me one time, "You can't expect people to be honest, nobody is that honest." We hear it on every side; "Everybody does it." So, we sign and date everything, have it notarized; lock it away in a safe box and keep our fingers crossed hoping nothing goes wrong.

To come close to appreciating the HOLINESS of God, we must get a new mind set. Nothing we have experienced or will ever experience can even come close to the holiness of God. Because we are finite and He is infinite. We may fear God's power and admire His wisdom, but we can merely stand in awe of His holiness.

Left to our own reasoning we will, for the most part, wind up trying to compare God to things we experience which will always fall short. We are totally dependent on this HOLY GOD to reveal himself. It took the Spirit of God to reveal the character of God. Man made in the image of God does have the ability to open up his mind to the hearing of the word and through the hearing of that word he can come to faith. *Rom.10.*

Holy is the way God is. To be holy He does not conform to some standard. He is the standard. We are tempted to question some of His actions because we being finite cannot always understand the reason behind His actions. But we need to be reminded He is absolutely holy with an infinite, incomprehensible holiness, and he is incapable of being other than holy. Because He is holy, all His other attributes are holy; that is, everything about this God is holy. It is not strange that the part of the temple where God promised to come and meet with His people; where the high priest would enter once each year with the blood sacrifice would be called *"The Most Holy Place."*

Perfect holiness is something that belongs to God alone. When we come to Him in faith He does give to us through the blood of His Son a measure of holiness in exchange for our filthy rags of sin. Paul described it this way:

> *"For He made Him who knew no sin to be sin for us, that we might become the righteousness of God in Him."*
> *(II Cor 5:21)*

We need not think this releases us from our duty to live holy lives. He said to Israel in the Old Testament and later in the New Testament to Christians, *"Be ye holy; for I am holy."* He did not say, be as holy as I am holy. Just because He did not command us to be as holy as He is does not release us from the duty to be as holy as we humans

138

can be. We are not free to ignore the instruction:

"Follow peace with all men, and holiness, without which no man shall see the Lord." (Heb 12:14)

Though man can never reach a state of holiness equal to God, he can live a lot better than he has been doing. Man has been telling himself for too long, "I'm just a sinner. God doesn't expect me to do any better, so don't worry about it." Yes, the Bible says "all have sinned and fall short of the glory of God". But God did not say, man had to sin because he could not help it. Some of the preaching I hear comes close to telling people this very thing. There are far too many examples of people in history who did live on a much higher plane and you and I know those today who are living on a much higher level. They have said no to the world and self and daily are taking up the cross to follow. The old excuse, "the devil made me do it" and "I just couldn't help it" won't cut it. As long as man keeps telling himself he can't, he is doomed to make very little improvement. Instead of saying "I can't" start saying "I can." You will be surprised at the difference.

139

Satan would have you believe there is no way out of your ungodliness. The message of the gospel, however, is that God has provided a covering of blood that washes us white as snow. When this holy God looks at us, He sees only our robe of righteousness which He has provided. We don't have to hide like Moses behind a rock but that blood is sufficient to cover all our sins. That is music to sinner's ears.

This God is so holy that no part of sin, however small we consider it to be, can dwell in His presence. This is why John, when describing that place where God is, said this:

> *"And the city had no need of the sun or of the moon to shine in it, for the glory of God illuminated it, and the Lamb is the light. And the nations of those who are saved shall walk in its light, and the kings of the earth bring their glory and honor into it........But there shall by no means enter it anything that defiles, or causes an abomination or a lie, but only those who are written in the Lamb's Book of Life."* (Rev 21:23-24,27)

We can submit to Him in humble obedience and continue to meditate on His holiness. We can love righteousness and hate iniquity. We can stay in communion with the Spirit of holiness and in fellowship with other saints while here on earth. By His grace, we will one day be ushered into the presence of this holy God never to depart.

Frederick W. Faber said it so well:

"How dread are Thine eternal years,
  O everlasting Lord!
By prostrate spirits day and night
  Incessantly adored!
How beautiful, how beautiful,
  The sight of Thee must be,
Thine endless wisdom, boundless power,
  And awful purity!
O how I fear Thee, living God!
With deepest, tenderest fears,
And worship Thee with trembling hope,
  And penitential tears." (Faber)

Also, Reginald Heber wrote:

"Holy, holy, holy! Lord God Almighty! Early in the morning our song shall rise to Thee."

And, **That's Good News!**

Chapter Thirteen

A GOD OF JUSTICE

"Righteousness and justice are the foundation
of Your throne; Mercy and truth go
before Your face."
(Ps 89:14)

"You have wearied the Lord with your words;
Yet you say, 'In what way have we wearied Him?'
In that you say, 'Everyone who does evil is good
in the sight of the Lord, And He delights in them,'
or, 'Where is the God of justice?'"
(Mal 2:17)

The first century world, like our world today, had lots of injustices. Ever since Adam and Eve thought they knew better than God what was good and what was evil, this world has been plagued with the problem. Even today those who like to call themselves atheist or agnostics try their best to show where the God of the Bible is unjust in some of His actions. They know if He is just in all His ways, then they have a harder time refusing to acknowledge Him. The one thing we hear people complaining about as much as anything is what they consider to be injustice. A preacher turned atheist wrote a book accusing the God of the Bible with being immoral, and he used the following argument about the man who was stoned to death for picking up sticks on the Sabbath.

"If there were something dangerous about picking up sticks on Saturday or Sunday, then humanity should know it by now. Since we all agree that such an act in itself is harmless, then whoever executes a person for committing such a "crime" is an immoral person. Even if there were something wrong about picking up sticks, it is not so terribly

144

wrong that it deserves capital punishment."

The problem with this man's argument is the same old problem. He does not understand who God really is. He seems to think that God must submit to his reason. Somehow disobeying this God's command is no more serious than violating some man-made speed limit which man has arbitrarily set. Man has never agreed with the justice of God. Man is imperfect, and God is perfect in all His ways. As long as man refuses to admit that God is perfect to the infinite degree, we will have a problem accepting many things He has said and done. That is why a correct understanding of who this God is is so fundamental. Picking up sticks was not that serious because there was something inherently wrong with picking up sticks but because God is God and man is not. Until we learn this lesson we are in rebellion.

God's justice and righteousness are closely related just as all His attributes are knit together and cannot be separated. In fact, they all support each other. For God to be just, He must be right and to be right, He must be just. This is why man is not free to take part of God and reject the other. Some people will gladly accept what they understand is a merciful God but not a God who deals in justice. They have difficulty understanding how the same God can be both at the same time.

Man has a tendency to think because we have difficulty being merciful and just, in fact we think it is impossible. When did you ever hear someone described as a merciful and just person? They have the same difficulty understanding how God is both merciful and just.

In a world filled with so much injustice; nations dealing unjustly with other nations; employers not being fair and just with employees; employees not doing a just day's work; business deals that are so unjust even our courts have ruled them criminal. A God who is just and perfect in all His ways stands as a beacon of hope. To know there really is One we can trust is a source of comfort, He will not make a promise that is not just and He will be just in the fulfillment. The reward for doing good is just and the punishment for doing evil is just. It has to be that way.

Paul assured the Jews in Romans chapter three that even though some of them did not have faith (could not be trusted) that God was still faithful. He could still be trusted. In fact he seems to say the more unfaithful (untrusting) they were; the more the faithful (just) God shines. The darker the room; the brighter the light shines. It is the one who is sick that welcomes the doctor when he comes.

Man needs a God who is perfectly just in his very nature not someone who will only be just when he feels like it and the circumstances call for it. I have heard people say "I don't want God to be just, I want Him to be merciful." I have also heard preachers say that God is merciful now, but in the Day of Judgment, He will be just. I think I understand what they are trying to say, but they don't understand how He can be just and merciful at the same time. This is the difference in God and man. Man has the ability to act in mercy when he is so motivated, but he can be so moved to forget all about mercy and act out of vengeance and at least thinks he is being just. But we must realize this God cannot act other than He is. He is just, period.

I am well aware of the emphasis given by a great segment of those who call themselves Christian that God is so loving, merciful and gracious that any mention of a just God falls on deaf ears. There is one popular writer who was answering a question someone had asked him. It went something like this: "My grandmother did not believe in God. As far as I know, she never read a

Bible, prayed or went to church. Is she going to heaven?" His response was, "Don't worry about her. Jesus wants her saved more than you, and He usually gets what He wants." It's true it would do no good for him to worry about his grandmother who is dead and gone. God is capable and will take care of all the judging. That kind of teaching, however, has led too many souls down a road of apathy. Something tells me the devil would be pleased with that kind of preaching.

The more I observe the divisions in the religious world, I am convinced it is the result of believing one or more ideas that are true. But we separate them and emphasize one truth to the exclusion of other truth. That's why we hear it said...there is some truth in all the different churches. But in reality, some truth may be half truth and we know what half truth is.

All the wickedness in this world cries out for justice. Something in man cries out 'how long will the wicked be allowed to get away with his wickedness?' Unless there is a God who can be trusted to balance the scales and right the wrongs, then something is lacking. This God we are talking about has assured us He is just, and He will make right the wrongs, and from all His other attributes we can trust He is both able and willing. He has even promised His children if you leave it to Me, I will take care of it. He says, "*Vengeance is mine, I will repay.*" Abraham prayed for his nephew Lot who was in Sodom when God was going to destroy the city. His prayer was based on the justice of God, he said, "*Will not the judge of the earth do right?*" I think Abraham was saying, "Lord, I don't know what You will do, but whatever it is it will be right." You may ask what God will do in some particular situation. I confess I may not know but whatever He does, I know it will be right. This is the kind of faith we can have in this God. Because He is just in His very nature, we can trust. That's what it means to walk by faith.

Some in the religious community seem to be confused. They ask how God can be both just and forgive sinners. If the wages of sin is death, how can God let the sinner go free and still be just? This is a very good question and God must have known man would ask it. In response, God has supplied the sufficient answer. He has paid the debt Himself. Listen to how Paul explains it:

> "*But now the righteousness of God apart from the law is revealed, being witnessed*

by the Law and the Prophets, even the righteousness of God, through faith in Jesus Christ, to all and on all who believe. For there is no difference; for all have sinned and fall short of the glory of God, being justified freely by His grace through the redemption that is in Christ Jesus, whom God set forth as a propitiation by His blood, through faith, to demonstrate His righteousness, because in His forbearance God had passed over the sins that were previously committed, to demonstrate at the present time His righteousness, that He might be just and the justifier of the one who has faith in Jesus."
(Rom 3:21-26)

We can fully trust in Him that He has paid the debt.

" Tis so sweet to trust in Jesus, just to take Him at His word. Just to rest upon His promise, just to know thus saith the Lord."
(words by Louisa M R Stead)

Let the wicked beware lest he think because he is not punished in this life, he has escaped justice. Two farmers were having a conversation one day. One was a believer and the other was not. The unbeliever said to the believer, "My crop is just as good as yours, so, you have no advantage as a believer." The believer replied, "God doesn't settle all the accounts at November harvest time."

God extends His gracious offer of perfect justice in Christ. If you refuse, rest assured the words of Paul are still operable:

> *"Do not be deceived, God is not mocked;*
> *for whatever a man sows, that he will*
> *also reap. For he who sows to his flesh*
> *will of the flesh reap corruption, but he*
> *who sows to the Spirit will of the Spirit*
> *reap everlasting life. And let us not grow*
> *weary while doing good, for in due*
> *season we shall reap if we*
> *do not lose heart."*
> *(Gal 6:7-9)*

And, **THAT'S GOOD NEWS!**

Chapter Fourteen

THE GOD OF MERCY

*"For the Lord is good; His **mercy** is everlasting, And His truth endures to all generations."*

(Ps 100:4)

*"And the tax collector, standing afar off, would not so much as raise his eyes to heaven, but beat his breast, saying, 'God, be **merciful** to me a sinner*

(Lk 18:13)

If we had the tongues of men and angels, we could not adequately tell of the mercy of this God. His justice upholds the order of the universe. All heaven and earth bow before His holiness. His mercy is too good to be true and it comes down to us through Jesus Christ and meets our greatest need. It gives us beauty for ashes and garments of praise for all of our sadness.

The Mercy Seat was In The Holy of Holies

The tabernacle in the Old Testament had three rooms. The outer court was where the people could gather. The holy place was where the priest performed their several duties. The inner part was called "The Most Holy Place." This was where the High Priest alone would enter once a year on the day of atonement. He would sprinkle the blood of the sacrificial lamb on what was called, "The Mercy Seat." This was that special place where only the High Priest, as a representative of the people, would meet with God and atonement would be made for the sins of the people. This was the extra special place where God had promised to meet with His people. Considering the character of this Holy God, it is fitting this special meeting place would be called "The Most Holy Place" and at the very center would be called, "The Mercy Seat." This "Mercy Seat" was so significant it was given special instructions for its construction in Exodus chapter twenty five:

> *"You shall make **a mercy seat** of pure gold; two and a half cubits shall be its length and a cubit and a half its width. And you shall make two cherubim of gold; of hammered work you shall make them at the two ends of the **mercy seat**. Make one cherub at one end, and the other cherub at the other end; you shall make the cherubim at the two ends of it of one piece with the **mercy seat**. And the cherubim shall stretch out their wings above, covering the mercy seat with their wings, and they shall face one another; the faces of the cherubim shall be toward the mercy seat. You shall*

*put the **mercy seat** on top of the
ark, and in the ark you shall put
the Testimony that I will give you.
And there I will meet with you,
and I will speak with you from
above the **mercy seat,** from
between the two cherubim which
are on the ark of the Testimony."*
(Ex 25:17-22a)

The human race would need so much mercy that in the very presence of God Himself in heaven a mercy seat would exist. This is the "Mercy Seat" where Jesus, as our high priest, would sprinkle His own blood as the "Once for all" atonement for the sins of all mankind. This is what allows us to come into the eternal presence of this holy God. The Hebrew writer explains it this way:

*"But Christ came as High Priest of the good
things to come, with the greater and more
perfect tabernacle not made with hands, that
is, not of this creation. Not with the blood of
goats and calves, but with His own blood He
entered the Most Holy Place once for all,*

having obtained eternal redemption."
(Heb 9:11-12)

*"But when the kindness and the love of God
our Savior toward man appeared, not by
works of righteousness which we have done,
but according to His* **mercy** *He saved us,
through the washing of regeneration and
renewing of the Holy Spirit."*
(Titus 3:3)

All the way from the Garden of Eden to the Isle of Patmos where Jesus dictated His final revelation through the angel to His servant John, the mercy of God runs deep. No serious student of scripture would argue otherwise. In one chapter of the book of Psalms, the writer repeats twenty six times, "His mercy endures forever." *(Ps 136)* No one knew better than the writer David how sweet is that mercy to the sinner. Perhaps this is why he repeated it so many times. Some things are so good to say it once is not enough. The apostle Paul in the New Testament seemed to feel the same way. His epistles are saturated with the concept of mercy. Listen to his words:

> *"But God, who is **rich in mercy,** because of*
> *His great love with which He loved us, even*
> *when we were dead in trespasses, made us*
> *alive together with Christ (by grace you*
> *have been saved, and raised us up together,*
> *and made us sit together in the heavenly*
> *places in Christ Jesus, that in the ages to*
> *come He might show the exceeding riches of*
> *His grace in His kindness toward us in*
> *Christ Jesus. For by grace you have been*
> *saved through faith, and that not of*
> *yourselves; it is the gift of God, not of*
> *works*, lest *anyone should boast."*
>
> *(Eph 2:4-9)*

The day will come when by His amazing grace we will be ushered into that eternal city and find ourselves in His presence.   There around the throne, with voices that will never grow tired praising the One who saved us, thanks and praise for His mercy will be on our lips. When we ask ourselves: Just what right do I have to be here? Deep down in our hearts we will know, this is not what we deserved. If we are honest, we must admit now that of our own selves we are bankrupt with nothing to pay. Even, *"when we have done all, we are still unprofitable servants."* Our only hope is mercy.

I visited with a man in prison who had killed his own mother. He admitted he was guilty and had been serving a life sentence and was coming up for parole. He had carried a heavy burden of guilt for many years. He said to me as we talked "I don't deserve to live; I deserved the electric chair but the judge gave me mercy." The more I thought about it we are all in the same boat; living on borrowed time granted by mercy.

Allow me to repeat: We need to forever banish from our minds the false notion that the God of the Old Testament was not a God of mercy. Mercy is another of His attributes that does not change. It has no beginning or end. To the sinner who has felt the burden of guilt, knowing that mercy is offered is truly good news! Take mercy out of the Bible and it would have to be rewritten from Genesis to Revelation.

Yes, this God is merciful. In the New Testament all His attributes are developed fuller. But one God speaks in both the Old and New

Testament, and what He speaks is the way He is. Whenever and wherever God manifest Himself to men, He acts like Himself. Whether in the Garden of Eden or the Garden of Gethsemane, God is merciful as well as just. He has always dealt in mercy with mankind and will always deal in justice when His mercy is despised. This He did in antediluvian times; thus He did when Jesus walked among men. His mercy flows freely today and will continue for no other reason than He is God.

We must be reassured that divine mercy is not a temporary mood that God may have from time to time. It is a part of His eternal being, and we need not fear that it will someday cease to be. His mercy, like all His attributes, has no beginning but has existed from all eternity. So it will never cease to be. It will never be more and it has never been less since it is infinite. Nothing that has occurred or will occur in heaven and earth or hell can change the tender mercies of God. Forever the boundless, overwhelming mercy of our God stands.

Judgment is God's justice poured out on man's rebellion. However, the mercy of God is His goodness extended to the guilty when they are repentant. When we repent and pray for mercy, we expect to receive. Not because we deserve it, but because mercy is an attribute of this God and is infinite in nature.

It is not enough to believe that God showed mercy in times past to other people. Unless I believe His mercy is extended to me, it's not the good news I need and it will have little effect in my life. I remember early in my life I had the idea that Jesus had died for the world as a whole. Then one day somewhere along the way it began to dawn on me that He died for me personally; as if I had been the only person in the world. That made it very personal for me and changed my life. His mercy is available to me right now in my present situation. Every day I receive His mercy; I don't get what I deserve.

"Arise my soul, arise;
shake off thy guilty fears;
The bleeding Sacrifice in my
behalf appears:
Before the throne my Surety stands,
My name is written on His hands.

160

My God is reconciled;

His pardoning voice I hear:

He owns me for His child;

I can no longer fear:

With confidence I now draw nigh,

And "Father, Abba, Father, cry"

(Charles Wesley, author)

God does not have stop and start buttons on His attributes. He does not stop one and start another. He is not like my computer; sometimes I have to go out of one program before another will work. God does not work like that.

God's mercy has been at work from the very beginning and was displayed at the cross for all to see. If anyone has ever had doubts concerning His mercy, all you have to do is look at the cross and what was done there. All we deserved was poured out on God's Son and mercy was made available to all who will come to Him.

All of who this God is was manifested in its glory at the cross. Here He showed His great power, the power to lay down His life and to take it up again. The love of God that surpasses knowledge was displayed for the entire world tosee; He said, "I love you this much." The ever presence of God was displayed; God came near. The justice of God was shown; this is what the sinner deserves. The mercy of God was manifested; the human race did not get what it deserved. Instead, the punishment was placed upon Him. Grace was freely bestowed, blessings above and beyond anything man could even imagine was made available by that cross.

No wonder the cross is the center of the Christian religion. No wonder Paul would say that he preached the cross as the *power of God and the wisdom of God.* And his only glory would be in the cross. It was at the cross that the mercy of God was shown to all. Instead of man receiving the just punishment for his sin, he was given mercy and Jesus took the punishment. When Jesus offered mercy to that dying thief, it was God acting like God.

The story goes that John Bowring was sailing past the coast of Macao, China. On the shore, there were the remains of an old, fire gutted church. Looking above all the ruins, he saw the

church's cross still standing. It is thought that this
scene served as the inspiration for this song. Its title was carved on Bowring's tombstone.

"In the Cross of Christ I glory,
Towering o-er the wrecks of time;
All the lights of sacred story,
Gathers round its head sublime.
When the woes of life o-er take me,
hopes deceive, and fears annoy,
Never shall the Cross forsake me:
Lo! It glow with peace and joy.
When the sun of bliss is beaming,
Light and love upon my way,
From the Cross the radiance streaming
Adds new luster to the day.
Bane and blessing, pain and pleasure,
By The Cross are sanctified;
Peace is there
That knows no measure,

163

Joys that thru all time abide,
(John Bowering, author)

"Mercy there was great and grace was free,
Pardon there was multiplied to me…"
(words from "At Calvary" by Wm R Newel)

One reason there will be no boasting in heaven is that all of us will understand we did not get what we deserved. And none will be able to claim they are more worthy than anyone else.

"And, **"That's Good News!"**

Chapter Fifteen

THE GOD OF GRACE

"For the grace of God that brings salvation has appeared to all men, teaching us that, denying ungodliness and worldly lusts, we should live soberly, righteously, in this present age, looking for the blessed hope and glorious appearing of our great God and Savior Jesus Christ."
(Tit 2:11-12)

"But may the God of all grace, who called us to His eternal glory by Christ Jesus, after you have suffered a while, perfect, establish, strengthen, and settle you. To Him be the glory and the dominion forever and ever. Amen."
(I Pet 5:10-11)

As I try to write a few pages on this wonderful attribute of our God, I feel like Paul did when he started that great chapter on love… *"If I had the tongues of men and of angels"*… I could not begin to tell the wonderful, marvelous, un-surpassing, greater than all our sin, amazing grace that is part of His very nature. Like all His other attributes, it knows no end. It lies at the very heart of the Christian faith. How anyone could possibly read His revelation to fallen man and not come away in awe of this attribute is a mystery.

There is good reason the song "Amazing Grace" is perhaps the most loved religious song. One good thing I notice the longer a person lives the Christian life, and the closer they seem to be to the Lord, the more they give praise for God's grace. The more we learn about the holiness, righteousness and the justice of God the more we see ourselves as we really are and our need for grace.

Man's greatest need is for mercy and grace. He needs mercy lest he get what he deserves. He needs grace to receive anything that is worthwhile. Grace, by its very nature, is always associated with good. If it's grace, it has to be good: we would never describe it any other way.

166

When we think about grace as something beyond anything we could ever earn, we think we need a modifier such as marvelous grace, amazing grace, and surpassing grace. Really, the grace of God is almost too good to be true. Before we go any farther perhaps we need to state some things grace is and some things grace is not.

Grace is the light that comes into human darkness to dispel guilt, fear and anxiety. Grace is the single word that expresses all that God has been about since before time began. God is love. God is light. God is truth. God is grace.

Grace is not a view of the God of the Bible as a sort of generic deity who is on par with a smorgasbord of the world's religions. Grace is not moral license that permits one to do his own thing without fear of God or compromising eternity. Grace is not a view of faith that says whatever floats your boat or gives you comfort regardless of its value is ok. Grace is not Jesus created in your image and with no obedience or accountability on our part. Grace is not faith that has no works and acts to validate. Grace is not an aversion to the simple command for baptism by the authority of Jesus for remission of sins, repented of with godly sorrow. Grace is not being a Christian and despising the church made up of fellow believers and community that nurtures your faith. Grace is not taking the blessings of the faith community without serving, giving, growing in the Lord and sharing the good news with others. Grace is not doing as I please and calling on Jesus' name making myself seem holy. Grace is not copping out on the call for repentance that shows itself in real life change. So many times when grace is discussed, whether we say it or not, this is the message some seem to hear.

Grace is not just something God does, but it is an integral part of His very nature. When we say this God is a God of grace, we are saying there is no way God cannot be gracious. God's grace is the same as in all His attributes. This is why He could say to the apostle Paul *"My grace is sufficient... Where sin abounds, grace much more abounds."* That was "Good News" to Paul and should be "Good News" to us.

John tells us in his gospel, *"For the law was given through Moses, but grace and truth came through Jesus Christ."(Jn 1:17)* Some have jumped to a wrong conclusion from this statement. They think Moses only knew law and Jesus only knew grace. Some have reached the conclusion that

168

the Old Testament is only a book of law and the New Testament is only a book of grace. Nothing could be farther from the truth. Early in the book of Genesis we read, *"But Noah found grace in the eyes of the Lord." (Gen 6:8).* The law that was given at Sinai had existed in the mind of God before there was ever a world. We might argue whether it was a law for the people before that time, but all the things stated in that Law came out of the very nature of God. It is not wrong to lie because it was written on tablets of stone by God. It is wrong to lie because it is an insult to the holy character of God.

Grace is developed more fully in the New Testament. It flows through Jesus and His sacrifice on the cross to bring salvation from sin to every nation. But grace has always been in the very nature of God and no sinner has ever returned to fellowship and favor with God except by grace. There has never, under either Old Testament or New Testament, been anything in the keeping of law that would earn sinful man the right to enter the presence of this holy God. Some have tried to say that keeping the Old Law was not good enough but keeping the New Law is good enough. Both are wrong. Here again some have jumped to a wrong

169

conclusion that there is no need to keep any law. Let me be very clear here: THERE HAS NEVER BEEN A TIME OR PEOPLE WHO ARE EXEMPT FROM THE HOLY LAW OF GOD. If that were the case, there is no reason for God to have given a law, and it would be meaningless. The truth is once man violated the law there is nothing in the law itself (old or new) that could atone for or forgive the sin. It took the unselfish, undeserving, gracious act of God himself when He sacrificed Himself on the Cross to take away the guilt of sin. That is what the gospel is all about. That's what the Christian religion is all about. The Christian religion hinges on the death, burial and resurrection of our Lord. Man did not do what he was supposed to have done. And now, regardless of what he might do he has no right to boast.

"But we are all like an unclean thing, and all our righteousness are like filthy rags; we all fade as a leaf, and our iniquities, like the wind, have taken us away." (Isa 64:6)

That statement declares the need of grace and that's in the Old Testament.

Because there has been considerable teaching on grace that has led to misunderstanding, there needs to be some explanation. How grace is applied and who receives grace needs to be understood. There are certain aspects of God's grace that are bestowed upon all mankind simply because they are a part of the human race. For instance: life is a gift from God that is unmerited. The sun shines on the earth and everyone enjoys it warmth. It rains on the just and the unjust. The rich fool's ground produced a bountiful crop. These are all what we might call temporal blessings, and they are all gifts of God's grace.

However, there is another area where the grace of God works a little different, but always in harmony with His other attributes. This is in the salvation of sinful man. The Bible tells us salvation is in Jesus Christ. Paul says *all spiritual blessings are in Christ. (Eph 1:3)* Grace bestowed in salvation is a spiritual blessing that is given freely to all in Christ. The grace of salvation is only promised to those in Christ. In Christ, all sins have been paid for by the sacrifice of Jesus, and God can give this grace and still remain true to all His other attributes. So when Paul wrote to the Ephesians:

"For by grace you have been saved through faith and that not of yourselves; it is the gift of God, not

171

of works lest anyone should boast."
(Eph 2:8)

He was writing to those who were in Christ. Some have tried to apply this to all; even those who are outside of Christ. I believe we can truthfully say, all God's grace for the salvation of mankind is in Christ. Outside of Christ, there is no grace when it comes to salvation from sin. Yes, evil men outside of Christ enjoy all His temporal blessings every day. But, if man wants salvation from sin, he must come into Christ where all that grace is. We can truthfully say, salvation from sin is not conditional but positional.

Is there a Bible story that illustrates this grace applied to a sinner? The story of David in the Old Testament is one of the greatest examples of grace. You can read his story in the book of II Samuel. God had taken David from minding his father's sheep and elevated him to King of Israel. David had done some noble things and God had given him many great victories over his enemies. Yet Satan was able to tempt him and he committed some great evil acts. He took the wife of one of his most trusted soldiers and committed adultery with her. He then had the soldier killed to try and cover

172

it up. By every law of justice David should have been hanged in the town square. Keep in mind God had struck people dead for what would be considered much less than this but look what He does for David: He tells him his sin is forgiven. He allows him to still reign as king. He allows him to keep the woman he had no right to. They had a son named Solomon who became king. He was permitted to be in the blood line of Jesus and promised his seed would always reign. Jesus is even called the "Son of David," an honor that could never have been deserved. God did bestow grace during Old Testament times.

The story of the prodigal son in Luke chapter fifteen tells just how gracious this God is to sinners today. Here was a boy who had for all practical purposes wished his father was dead. To ask for your inheritance early was a death wish. The father was gracious to give him his inheritance. What did he do? He took a journey to a far country. Notice he doesn't invest it in something, but he wastes it. He doesn't just waste it, but wastes it with harlots. When it is all gone, he still is too stubborn to admit his wrong, so he hires out to a foreigner to feed pigs. Pigs were considered unclean animals. Not only was this boy feeding pigs but was eating the same food. This young man has fallen as low as you could fall.

When he does come to himself and comes crawling back home, what does the father do? The young man admits he is not worthy to even be called his son. The best he could hope for would be hired as a servant. By all rights he deserved to be banished forever from the presence of his father and the rest of the family. If he ever showed his face near the place, he would be arrested and charged with trespassing. Everything this young man received was grace. The father running to greet him with a hug and a kiss; receiving the best robe to wear; given shoes for his feet; wearing the family ring. The fatted calf was killed and a party thrown in his honor.

Because this young man came to his senses in that pig pen; because he walked the long distance to get back home; because he tries to apologize for his actions; because he offered to work as a hired hand, doesn't merit him any of his father's blessings. Everything his father did was grace and every day thereafter that young man would surely be grateful.

Let us beware lest we think for a moment that by

coming to Christ in faith, confessing His Name, and turning from our wicked ways, and being baptized that we somehow earned salvation. We have only come to Him where all these blessings are. If you could earn it, it would not be grace.

All God's attributes are amazing, marvelous, wonderful and beyond our comprehension. But we sing of His grace more than anything.

> *Amazing grace! how sweet the sound! that saved a wretch like me! I once was lost, but now I'm found; was blind but now I see.*
>
> *Wonderful grace of our loving Lord! Marvelous grace that is greater than all our sin! Just to know that His grace reaches me!*

Before the inspired writer would wash his quill and lay it aside for the last time he would write this last line:

> *"The grace of our Lord Jesus Christ be with you all. Amen."*
> *(Rev 22:21)*

And, **That's Good News!**

175

Chapter Sixteen

THE GOD WHO LOVES

For God so loved the world that He gave His only begotten Son, that whoever believes in Him should not perish but have everlasting life."
(John 3:16)

"In this is love, not that we loved God, but that He loved us and sent His Son to be the propitiation for our sins."
(I Jn 4:10)

"He who does not love does not know God, for God is love."
(I Jn 4:8)

An interesting headline appeared in the Nashville Tennessean a few years ago. It read: IMAGE OF GOD OFTEN DEPENDS ON WHERE YOU LIVE. The article talked about how people in different sections of the country have such differing ideas of what God is like. These conclusions were based on a survey done by Baylor University.

In the West, the survey said people perceived God as distant, remote, and uninvolved. Why? Under the big western sky, the vast silences lead to lonely stoicism.

In the Midwest, a benevolent image of God dominates. The reason: people are friendly and family oriented. An annual farm belt bounty reminds people of divine blessings.

In the East, a critical God prevails. God sees and judges; refuses to comfort rescue or punish. The writer seems to guess: The region's population density, high rents and dark winters create an ethic of nervous striving.

In the South, pollsters find an Authoritarian God- one who is judgmental, active, and angry at sin. Explanation: It is blamed on an attitude resulting in the guilt and brutality of slavery, Civil War and poverty. Certain passages from scripture: Adam and Eve, Paul, and Revelation were focused on. But there was not focus on the Sermon on the Mount. The writer goes on to talk about how these images of God effect how people think and act in their everyday life and yes, it affects their politics.

The article concluded by saying the question that diplomats, generals and presidents should be asking each other is: "What image of God do you worship and why?"

This article brings to focus how diverse and even confusing the concept of God is among the people of a nation that calls itself Christian. This tells me this effort is overdue. It also says a lot about how people have formed their image of God based not on His revelation of Himself but from the circumstances they find themselves in or in their special environment. It stands as an indictment of our religious teaching institutions who have failed miserably in this area. First things have not been first.

In I John 4:8 the apostle John declares *"God is love."* Some have taken these words as the only description of God. They go on to think; God is what love is. They reason, if God is love, then love is God. If God is equal to love, then love and God are identical. This kind of reasoning corrupts the true personality of God and does away with all his attributes, save one. The god we end up with is not the true God but a substitute. We say that God is light; that Christ is the way, the truth and the light. We say that a man is kindness itself, but we are not saying that the man and kindness is the same thing.

When we say that God is love, we are saying that love is an essential part of His nature. It expresses the way God is in the same way the words holiness, justice, and mercy do. Remember, God never suspends one of His attributes in order for another to act. God always acts like himself.

John 3:16 is the golden text of the Bible as far as most Bible readers are concerned. Surely, it is a center piece of Scripture that expresses the very heart of God. However, it has been abused and misused in many ways. I have long described the Bible a lot like a large puzzle. If you take one small piece of a puzzle and try to interpret it all by itself you will almost always miss its significance. But if you can find where and how it fits into the overall picture, then you learn the real importance of that small piece. To find where that small piece fits in the puzzle does not diminish its importance but rather enhances it.

Only with some understanding of the overall

picture that surrounds John 3:16 will we understand it. Only when we see all the attributes of God together will we understand the real importance of each individually.

I would never want to understate the importance of this verse and the central importance of how the love of God is perhaps the greatest motivating force. We, as humans, are moved to action by love more than anything else. We are moved to love God in return when we come to understand He loved us first in spite of the fact we are sinners and undeserving of that love. A realization of this love even aids us in our love for our fellowman. There is a reason the command to love our neighbor comes after the command to love God. It really is the second commandment and not the first.

I want us to see how the love of God in no way overrides all His other attributes but how they all work together. His love compliments all His other attributes and all His other attributes compliment His love. From the other attributes of God, we learn something about His love. For instance, God is self-existence, so, his love is self existent. It is not dependent on any outside force. That is why His love is unconditional. God is eternal. Therefore,

His love is without end. God is infinite. Therefore, His love is without limits. God is holy. Therefore, his love is pure. No wonder Paul would write to the Ephesians:

"That you being rooted and grounded in love, may be able to comprehend with all the saints what is the breadth and height and length and depth and the height- to know the love of Christ which passes knowledge; that you may be filled with all the fullness of God."
(Eph 3:17b-19)

He seems to be encouraging them to understand the breadth; the height and depth of something that is beyond knowledge. It's easy to see he is saying this is what you reach for. Like a child who can never reach the star but by reaching toward that star that child will become better. The more we learn of God the more something inside us desires to love Him because He first loved us. So we stretch with all our might to reach that "unreachable star" along with others who are striving to reach for it also.

Of all His attributes, it is His love for us that will impact our everyday lives more than anything else. If we had all power as finite beings, we would not use it properly. The history of mankind shows that even a small amount of power corrupts many. If we were sovereign, we lack the wisdom to exercise it. But love is an attribute we do seem capable of putting to good use. It acts as a guiding light for the road of life and serves as a compass lest we get off course. Love will nudge us in the right direction and restrain us when we would go wrong. Paul would say in that chapter on love, if we don't possess it, anything we endeavor will be a failure.

God possesses a perfect love which operates in perfect harmony with all His other attributes. Perfect love works perfectly with perfect justice. His perfect righteousness is not compromised by His perfect love. His holiness is only enhanced by His perfect love. I like to describe this love like an overcoat where all of God is wrapped up in this coat of love. This is the way He wants us to be. Everything we believe, everything we do, everything we say, needs to be overcoated with love which John tells us will *cover a multitude of sins*. Paul told the Colossians:

"Let your speech always be with grace, seasoned with salt, so that you may know how you ought to answer each one."
(Col 4:6)

The question we hear repeated most by skeptics is "If God is a loving God, then how _____." You fill in the blank. The difficulty for believers to counter such questions is also failure on our part. Satan knows if he can convince men God is not a loving God, they will not want to serve Him. What is true of His love, the same is true with all His attributes. This is where the infinite is so different from the finite. We find ourselves fighting with ourselves, one part of our nature against another, but this God is not at war with Himself. The finite is so limited and the infinite is without limits. It cannot be confined within borders. This is why He can love the vilest of sinners just the same as the greatest saint who ever lived. This is why Paul could say:

"I am persuaded that neither death, nor life, nor angels, nor principalities nor powers, nor things present, nor things to come, nor height, nor depth

nor any other creature, shall be able
to separate us from the love of God,
which is in Christ Jesus our Lord."
(Rom 8:38-39)

This kind of love is beyond our understanding, much less our ability to ever attain it.

We may never understand perfectly what love is, but we can know how it manifests itself, and that is sufficient. Love always wills the good for all and never wills harm to anyone. This explains the words of John when he said, *"There is no fear in love."* Fear arises when we think some harm may come to us. We have no fear of those we are convinced love us. Perfect love does cast out fear. Truly the man who knows the love of God can have the peace of mind that passes all understanding. The world is full of groups who are at war with one another. Nations arm themselves with nuclear weapons because they think other nations don't love them. We lock our doors at night because we fear those we think hate us. It feels like the best we can hope for is that the law of averages is in our favor for survival. Depending on our ability to out-maneuver or out-think our enemies gives us reason to be afraid. But to know the love of God and to lean upon His arm, this and only this can cast out fear. Let a man become convinced that nothing can harm him and fear vanishes. A nervous reflex to pain may be felt at times, but the deep torment of fear is gone. God is love and God is sovereign. His love causes him to desire our everlasting good. Because He is sovereign, He can guarantee it.

We desperately need an understanding and acceptance of this love. Without it we may coat over and camouflage our fear for a while, but the least little disappointment comes along and that fear will raise its ugly head again.

Martin Luther expressed it this way in that beautiful hymn:

> *"The body they may kill;*
> *Gods truth abideth still,*
> *His kingdom is forever."*
> *(from "A mighty Fortress")*

In spite of the fact we are the offenders, God tells us that he is friendly and loves us. The first thing

He wants from us in return is that we love Him. We read the history of how man turned up his nose against the God who had created him. And for all practical purpose said, I'll do what I want to do whether You like it or not. This God did not love man any less. Everything He has done since that time has been to show His love and to bring man back. In spite of that fact, man did not want to be friends with God. His word assures us that He wants us to be his friends. God called Abraham His friend. Abraham did not claim first to be the friend of God. The disciples did not claim first to be friends of Jesus, but Jesus called to them and said, *"You are my friends."* Friends are supposed to love each other, but the sad news is in many cases man has turned it into a one way love by refusing to love in return.

Love has an emotional identification. It considers nothing its own but desires to freely give to the object of its affection. Acts of self sacrifice come natural to the one who loves. It was Jesus, who said:

> *"Greater love hath no man than this that a man lay down his life for his friend."*

We know when we allow ourselves to become emotionally attached to someone; we risk being hurt if they reject our love. I'm not sure to what extent this may apply to God, but being the all-knowing God, He must have known that part of His creation would reject His love. Still He has allowed His heart to become emotionally attached to us.

Even though He is self-cient, He doesn't need our love. Though He is self-existent, if we did not exist He would still be the same, yet, he wants our love. Remember this: If we love Him or hate Him He is still the same…He does not change. Though he is completely free, yet He has let His heart be bound to us forever; this love will never leave us.

> *"Herein is love, not that we loved God, but that he loved us and sent his Son to be a propitiation for our sins."* *(I Jn 4:10)*

One characteristic of love is that it takes pleasure in its object. God enjoys His creation. He looked upon everything He had made and said, "It is good." The love of God is one of the great realities of the universe. The hope of the world rests upon

the pillar of His love. It is a personal and intimate thing.   God   does   not love populations, He loves
people. He does not love masses, but individuals.
He loves us with a mighty love that has no beginning and can have no end. This is amazing. It's too good to be true. In the presence of such love we stand in awe. We sing of His love. We thank Him for it in our prayers, but only in eternity will we be able to fully extol it. Mankind's greatest need today is to come to know of this love and to respond in a fitting way. A half hearted response such as, "I'm not interested at this time. I'll think about it and let you know" would surely be an insult. This is not one of those things you put on the back burner.

"Thou shall love the Lord thy God with all
your heart and with all thy soul and with
all your mind, and the second is like it:
You shall love your neighbor as
yourself."
(Mt 22:37,39)

"We love Him because He first loved us."
(1John 4:19)

Who is this God?

John J. Whitttier wrote these words
:*Immortal love forever full, forever flowing free,
forever shared, forever whole, a never ebbing
sea. We may not climb the heavenly steeps, to bring
the Lord Christ down. In vain we search the lowest
deeps, for Him no depths can drown. But
warm, sweet tender, even yet a present help is He;
And faith has still its Olivet and love its Galilee.
The healing of His seamless dress is by our beds of
pain. We touch Him in life's throng and press and
we are whole again. Through Him the first fond
prayers are said. Our lips of childhood frame; the
last low whispers of our dead are burdened with
His pain."*

F.M. Lehman wrote the words:
*"The love of God is greater far than tongue or pen
can ever tell, it goes beyond the highest star
and reaches to the lowest hell. The guilty pair,
bowed down with care, God gave His Son to win.
His erring child He reconciled, and pardoned from
the sin. Could we with ink the ocean fill and were
the sky of parchment made. Were every stalk on
earth a quill, and every man a scribe by trade; to
write the love of God above would drain the ocean*

189

*dry; Nor could the scroll contain the whole, though
stretched from sky to sky. Oh, the love of God how
rich and pure! How measureless and strong.
It shall forever more endure –
the saints and angels song."*

All the attributes of God were manifested in Jesus as He showed us the Father. But from our human position, we are perhaps more able to make connection with the love shown to us in the way He lived and the death He died, than any other. If that love does not touch us we will certainly not be touched by His other attributes. If this all-powerful, all-wise, self-sufficient, self-existent, controller of life, gracious, just, merciful God did not love us, we would be no better off than if we had no God at all. His love is what rounds out and completes the circle that meets our every need. Likewise, it is our sincere love for Him that must undergird all of our devotion to Him. Otherwise, our service is vain.

And, **That's Good News!**

Chapter Seventeen

THE WISE GOD

"And God saw everything that He had made, and behold, it was very good."
(Gen 1:1)

"Because the foolishness of God is wiser than men, and the weakness of God is stronger than men."
(1Cor 1:25-26)

"If any of you lacks wisdom, let him ask of God, who gives to all liberally and without reproach, and it will be given to him."
(Jas 1:5)

When God revealed the dream of Nebuchadnezzar king of Babylon to Daniel, he cried:

> *"Blessed is the name of God forever and ever: for wisdom and might are His and He changed the times and the seasons: He removes kings, and setteth up kings: He gives wisdom to the wise and knowledge to them that know understanding. He revealeth the deep and secret things: He knoweth what is in the darkness and the light dwells in Him."*
>
> *(Dan 2:20-22)*

God's invisible qualities, His eternal power and divine nature can be clearly seen in His creation since time began. God has given us the revelation of Himself in order that we might know something of His inner nature; how He thinks; what His feelings are toward us and what He expects of us in return. If He had not given us this revelation, we would never have known these wonderful truths that are so important to our well being here and any hope we might have for life hereafter. These things

192

nature could never teach us. This is the purpose of His revelation in what we know as the Bible. All living creatures have been given life by God, and He wants everything to give glory to Him by acknowledging that He is wise and following His ways. All creatures in the animal world do give glory to Him by each fulfilling the purpose for which they were created. However, mankind is the one creature that is given the power of choice. It is God's desire that man, who is created in His image, would choose freely to bring glory to Him. It seems clear that this brings greater glory to God and even the angels in heaven are made to rejoice when this takes place. Wise men through the ages have accepted the fact that God is wise. Fools have been in denial. The Bible writers seem not to ask for or offer proof of His wisdom or power. It is enough for them to just state that He is wise and that He is God.

When we say that man or woman is wise, it seems sufficient. However, when we say that God is wise, the words seem so weak, and unable to convey the full weight of what we are trying to say. David said, *"His understanding is unique."*

Since the word infinite describes what is unique, it can have no modifiers. We do not say, "more unique" or "very infinite". In the presence of infinite (unlimited) wisdom, we stand in awe and silence. We realize for our God to be complete, He must be infinitely wise. The root cause of sin in the Garden was when Adam and Eve began to question the wisdom of God.

God has given those created in His image a degree of wisdom which is sufficient to accomplish his work in this life. We are not a mass of zombies wandering aimlessly in this world. Man has, by the exercise of this limited wisdom given to him, accomplished some marvelous things. However, this wisdom has severe limits. When compared to the unlimited wisdom of God, it is so small. If we refuse to acknowledge our Maker is not just wise, but He is wisdom in the perfect sense. We lower ourselves to the level of the beast of the field.

Wisdom in the Bible is always above the normal. Whether speaking of God or men it is always considered the highest moral standard. It is always conceived as being pure, loving and good. Shrewdness that is sometimes mistaken for wisdom is in most instances attributed to those who are evil. This is not true wisdom but false. These two kinds of wisdom are in conflict. In fact the history of the world can be seen as a contest between the wisdom of God and the cunning of Satan and fallen man. This is one reason the outcome is not in doubt. The imperfect will ultimately fall before the perfect. God has warned that he will *take the wise in their own craftiness and bring to nothing the understanding of the prudent.*

Wisdom is the ability to devise perfect ends and to achieve those ends by perfect means. Perfect wisdom sees the end from the beginning. It sees everything in perfect focus. It sees every part as it relates to the whole. Because He is perfect in wisdom, every act has been a perfect act; every thought has been a perfect thought. Every thing He has done has been perfect for His own glory and for our greatest good. All His acts are as pure as they are wise, and as wise and they are pure. Not only could His acts not be done better; a better way of doing them could not be imagined. An infinitely wise God must work in a manner not to be improved upon by finite creatures. The Psalmist declared:

"O Lord, how manifold are they works, in wisdom has thou made them all. The earth is full of Your possessions."(Ps. 104:24)

195

Unbelievers through the ages have argued they could not believe in the basic wisdom of a world where so much appears to be so wrong. The believer's view is more realistic. It is that this world is not at the moment the best of all possible worlds. It is a world suffering from a calamity. It is the result of a stubborn rebellious race. Sin has entered into the world. The Bible states, *"The whole creation now groans and travails"* because it too suffers from the shock of man's rebellion. He described it this way in another place:

"Creature was made subject to vanity
(not willingly) but by reason of Him
who has subjected the same in hope."
(Rom 8:20)

No effort is made here to justify the ways of God with man; just a simple statement of fact. God and His character is its own best defense.

In spite of all the pain, suffering death and tears that plagues us in this existence, there is hope. This God we believe in is infinitely wise and good. So we like Abraham (who is called "the Father of the faithful") *"do not waiver at the promise through unbelief, but with strong faith, giving glory to God,*

196

and being fully persuaded that He is able to perform what He has promised."(Rom 4:21-22) We base our hope in God alone and we willingly submit to a walk by faith and not by sight. If He is what He is, He is enough. This alone is true faith. Faith that is not real must be supported by that which the eye can see; a faith that needs some kind of a feel good or touch; a faith that science and human philosophy must agree with or always be supported by some archeological discovery. Remember Jesus' words to Thomas who refused to believe until he could see the nail prints in His hands and the hole in His side.

> *"Because you have seen Me, you have believed. Blessed are those who have not seen and yet have believed."*
> *(Jn 20:29b)*

The plan for the redemption of mankind though the sending of His Son was one of the wise acts of God.

> *"Without controversy great is the mystery of godliness: God was manifest in the flesh, justified in the Spirit, seen of angels, preached unto the Gentiles,*

197

believed on in the world, received
up into glory."
(I Tim 3:16)

Woe to us should we try to suggest that any improvement could be made in the divine procedure.

It is vitally important that we hold the truth of God's infinite wisdom as a central part of our faith. To hold this faith in our hearts is not enough. For,

Faith without works is dead being alone."
(James 2:20)

Our faith must be put into practice and made a part of everyday living. God promised His people:

"I will go before you, and make the
crooked places straight: I will break in
pieces the gates of brass, and cut
asunder the bars of iron: and I will give
thee the treasures of the darkness, and
hidden riches of the secret places, that
thou mayest know that I, the Lord,
which call thee by thy name, am

the God of Israel.''
(Isa 45:2-3)

James said:
"If any man lack wisdom, let him
ask of God.''
(James 1:5a)

"For the wisdom of this world is
foolishness with God. For it is written,
"He catches the wise in their
own craftiness.''
(I Cor 3:19)

The battle that has raged since that encounter of Satan with the woman in the garden is basically whether to follow the Word of this wise God or listen to the false message of Satan. The battle that rages in the heart of every soul today is the same. Will we follow this wise God or the foolish things the god of this world tells us?

Jesus told the story of a certain rich man whose ground produced a bountiful crop. He had to make a decision about what to do because his barns were not large enough to store it all. He decided to tear down the old barns and build larger ones. Then he said:

"Soul, you have many goods laid up for many years; take your ease; eat, drink and be merry. But God said to him, "You fool!"
(Lk 12:18)

Paul recognized this struggle was going on even among some Christians in the church at Corinth when he wrote to them.

"Because the foolishness of God is wiser than men, and the weakness of God is stronger than men. Glory only in the Lord for you see your calling, brethren, that not many wise according to the flesh, not many mighty, not many noble, are called. But God has chosen the foolish things of the world to put to shame the wise, and God has chosen the weak things of the world to put to shame the things which are mighty; and the base things of the world and the things which are despised God has chosen, and the things which are not, to bring to nothing the things that are, that no flesh should glory in His presence."
(I Cor 1:25-27)

200

"But of Him you are in Christ Jesus, who became for us wisdom from God and righteousness and sanctification and redemption that, as it is written, 'He who glories, let him glory in the Lord.'"
(I Cor 1:30-31)

The Spirit must have known man would be tempted to think his own wisdom was the highest. So, man needed to realize his wisdom is foolishness when compared to the infinite wisdom of this God. This is why for man to boast in the presence of this God is pride at its worst. Jesus would say, the wise man is the one who builds his house (life) on the solid rock (teachings of this wise God) and when the storms come his house will stand. In contrast, the fool is one who follows his own way and in the storm his house will fall.
(taken from the Sermon on the Mount...Matt 7)

"Trust in the LORD with all your heart, And lean not on your own understanding; In all your ways acknowledge Him, And He shall direct your paths. Do not be wise in your own eyes; Fear the LORD and depart from evil. It will be

*health to your flesh, And strength
to your bones.”
(Prov 3:5-8)*

*“Honor the LORD with your possessions,
And with the first fruits of all your
increase so your barns will be filled
to overflowing and your vats will brim
over with new wine.”
(Prov 3:9-10)*

*“Now to the King eternal, immortal, invisible, to
God who alone is wise, be honor and glory
forever and ever. Amen.”
(I Tim 1:17)*

Modern man has made great advances in science and technology but the words of the prophet of old are still true. This would be a good starting place for us. *“O LORD, I know the way of
man is not in himself;
It is not in man who walks to direct
his own steps.”
(Jer 10:23)*

God can be trusted because He is wise.

And, **THAT'S GOOD NEWS!**

202

Chapter Eighteen

GOD WHO SEEKS THE LOST

"The Lord is not slack concerning His promise, as some men count slackness, but is longsuffering toward us, not willing that any should perish but that all should come to repentance."
(II Pet 3:9)

"For the son of Man is come to seek and save that which was lost."
(Lk 19:10)

203

Have you ever thought about this? If someone held a gun to your head and told you to hand over all your Bibles and you could only keep one chapter of one Bible, which chapter would you choose to keep? I realize that any chapter we might choose would depend on the rest of the Bible for much of our understanding of a lot of that chapter. Knowing what you know about the Bible as a whole, surely there is one chapter that has a special place in your heart, and you personally would want to keep it close. Perhaps you feel that one chapter is a short summary of the whole.

There are several chapters I would wrestle with if I had to choose one to keep for my own personal encouragement. I think of the lost world out there and unless they come to the realization, they are lost. This God, first and foremost, wants to save them. Based on this, I believe there is a chapter that displays in a marvelous way the number one thing on the heart of this God; which is, His love for the lost.

Have you ever thought about what it is that God spends most of the time doing and for what reason? Of course, God is not anyway affected by time, but let me tell you what I am convinced this God has on His mind more than anything. If it were possible for us to call and ask God "What's on Your mind today?" His reply would be, *"That lost sheep, lost coin, lost prodigal and lost elder brothers. I won't sleep till every lost one is found and saved."*

I read of how man chose to listen to the serpent instead of God in the garden. This caused the great separation of the human race from this holy God. Then how, from that moment in time, everything this God has done has been with one thing in mind. Bring lost man back into fellowship with Him.

Someone might say this is not an attribute of God, but something He does. However, everything God does is because that's the way He is. We could say He seeks the lost because of all His attributes. Everything in His nature moves Him to do what He does and what He does is seek the lost. We are not interested in splitting theological hairs. We want to deal more with the practical. Nothing is more practical than His number one mission of seeking the lost. Everything He has done, what He is doing and will do must be understood as it relates to His main mission. Seeking the lost is the natural thing you would expect this God to do.

The plan in the mind of God before there was a world was not to establish some earthly kingdom where He would rule from the city of Jerusalem.

His plan called for the Son, a part of the Godhead Himself, to bruise the head of the Serpent and make atonement for man's sins. This would bridge the gap for you and me to return to fellowship with Him.

From much preaching on the airways today, you would think God is more interested in the Jews going back to the land of Palestine than anything else. There is one group whose work is raising money for transportation for Jews who are living in other countries to travel to Israel.

From my reading of the Bible, God's bringing the Jews into the land of Palestine in the first place was to bring a Savior into the world so that all men would have the opportunity for salvation. Once that Savior came, the whole purpose for that special nation of people was fulfilled. When they rejected their Savior they rejected the whole purpose for which they were chosen and Jesus told them *"Your house is left desolate." (Matt 23:38)* Now where a Jew or Gentile lives is not important. He wants both to come to faith in His Son and be saved. Paul declared:

"As many as have been baptized into Christ have put on Christ and in Christ there is neither Jew nor

*Greek, bond or free, male or female and all who
are in Christ are Abraham's seed and heirs
according to the promise."
(Gal 3)*

A full discussion of this would require an additional volume.

It is not strange that Luke would describe the mission of Jesus is: *"to seek and save that which was lost."(Lk 19:10b)* But men were not interested in a Savior. They wanted a Messiah who would save them from political bondage. They wanted a Messiah who would feed all the hungry people. They wanted a Messiah who would restore the kingdom as it had been in the days of David and Solomon. Perhaps this is why Satan offered Him the kingdoms of this world and challenged Him to turn stones into bread in the temptation. If only He would forget about going to that cross.

So, it's not strange that the angel would announce at His birth that He was the One *"who would save His people from their sins." (Matt 1:21b)* It's not strange that Luke would say, *"This Man receives sinners." (Lk 15:2b).* He himself would declare, *"I came not to call the righteous, but sinners." (Matt 9:13)*

207

Let's take an indepth look at that chapter I was talking about. It explains so well in parable form the plan and purpose of God and how He feels about the lost.

Luke Chapter fifteen

Jesus was being surrounded by what was considered the worst of sinners. Some were the tax collectors and outcast of that day. The religious elite were outraged that this One who claimed to be the Messiah would lower Himself to associate with such a crowd. In response to their murmuring, Jesus told a series of parables which have served as text for many sermons and even books through the ages. Under the umbrella of these three parables can be seen the whole of humanity, their lost condition, and how this God feels about them all.

Jesus puts them in the form of questions:

"What man of you, having a hundred sheep, if he loses one of them, does not leave the ninety-nine in the wilderness, and go after the one which is lost till he finds it? And when he has found it, he lays it on his shoulders, rejoicing. And when he comes home he calls together his friends and neighbors, saying to them, 'rejoice with me, for I have found

208

my sheep which was lost!'

Or what woman, having ten silver coins, if she lose one coin, does not light a lamp, sweep the house, and seek diligently until she find it? And when she has found it, she calls her friends and neighbors together, saying, 'Rejoice with me, for I have found the piece which I lost!'

Jesus continued: *"A certain man had two sons. And the younger of them said to his father, 'Father, give me the portion of goods that falls to me.' So he divided to them his livelihood. And not many days after, the younger son gathered all together, journeyed to a far country, and there wasted his possessions with prodigal living.*

But when he had spent all, there arose a severe famine in the land, and he began to be in want. Then he went and joined himself to a citizen of that country, and he sent him into his fields to feed swine. And he would gladly have filled his stomach with the pods that the swine ate, and no one gave him anything. But when he came to himself, he said, 'How many of my father's hired servants have bread enough and to spare, and I perish with hunger! I will arise and go to my father, and will say to him, 'Father, I have sinned against heaven *and before you and I am no longer worthy to **be** called your son. Make me like one of your hired servants.'*

And he arose and came to his father. But when he was still a great way off, his father saw him and had compassion, and ran and fell on his neck and kissed him. And the son said to him, 'Father, I have sinned against heaven and in your sight, and am no longer worthy to be called your son.'

But the father said to his servants, 'Bring the best rob and put it on him, and put a ring on his hand and sandals on his feet. And bring the fatted calf here and kill it, and let us eat and be merry; for this my son was dead and is alive again; he was lost and is found.' And they began to be merry.

Now the older son was in the field, And he came and drew near to the house, he heard music and dancing. So he called one of the servants and asked what these things meant. And he said to him, 'Your brother has come, and because he has received safe and sound, your father has killed the fatted calf.' But he was angry and would not go in. therefore his father came out and pleaded with him. So he answered and said to his father, 'Lo, these many years I have been serving you; I never transgressed your commandment at any time; and yet you never gave me a young goat, that I might make merry with my friends. But as soon as this son of yours came, who has devoured your livelihood with the harlots, you have killed the fatted calf for him.' And he said to him, 'Son, you are always with me, and all that I have is yours. It was right that we should make merry and be glad, for your brother was dead and is alive again, and was lost and is found.'"

There are so many lessons in these stories. I think Jesus was challenging them in the first two stories; this is what you would do if you lost a sheep or a coin. You would leave no stone unturned to recover them and you would gladly throw a party to celebrate. They would gladly attend the party for either the lost sheep or lost coin. But the lost boy was a different story.

Could it be that Jesus was giving an overall picture of a lost world? Could He be saying, there are lost sheep, there are lost coins, there are lost boys, and each is different?

Are some lost like sheep? Sheep are lost not because they want to be lost. I am told that sheep have no sense of direction, if they get out of sight of the other sheep they don't know which way to go. This is why the shepherd had to leave the other sheep and go searching for it. He could not just sit and wait for the sheep to find its way back.

In one sense, all sinners are lost like sheep. Yes, the prophet Isaiah said, *"All we like sheep who have gone astray."* As sheep, we may know we are lost but don't know our way back. Certainly man does not have the power to save himself. This is why it took the first move on the part of God Himself. So unless God had come searching for lost man, he would have been forever doomed. It might even be said that some are lost and have no idea how they became lost or what to do about it. Consider the question asked by the man from Ethiopia in Acts chapter eight verse thirty one who was reading his Bible. He was asked if he understood what he was reading. He answered, *"How can I accept unless someone guide me."* It was not just an academic exercise when Jesus commanded His disciples to go and teach all nations. Unless they hear they cannot believe and unless they believe they cannot be saved. (Rom 10:10-15)

Are some lost like a coin? The coin was lost because of the carelessness of someone else. The

212

coin did not just decide one day it did not like being in the woman's purse, so it went rolling around. Also, the coin would never have found its way back into circulation. Thus, the need for someone to search. God is that woman who would not sleep till every crack and corner, every rug had been turned upside down and the coin was found and the party followed. Let me just add here, there is a great need for searchers today for many lost coins. Where are those who are willing to light a candle, get a broom, and start sweeping? How many children are lost because parents made no effort to show them the way to Jesus while they were young and now someone else must do the searching? Is it any wonder Jesus would say, *"The harvest is great but the labors are few."* Christians, our task is clear, and the work has just begun.

For sure many are lost like the younger son. He seemed to know exactly what he was doing. No, he didn't expect the results He got, but he knew he was wrong. He knew his father loved him. He just knew he wanted what he wanted and he wanted it now. Our world today seems to have a lot who fit this description. They say, "I want what I want and I want it now; I don't care if it's right or wrong." They have adopted the beer slogan "I only go around once, so I want to get all the gusto I can."

This group for the most part is well aware where they went wrong. They know when they turned their nose up at God and said, "Bye, bye. I'm going to the far country. Don't call me, I'll call you." Most of these will only return when they come to themselves. And it's sad, but many will not come to themselves until they have spent all and have fallen into the pigpen. For some, it takes financial ruin. For others, the doctor will come in and say, "The cancer is inoperable." I have heard people pray, "Lord may something be said or done that will bring someone to repentance." I have asked myself: do they really know what they may be asking for? How often have we heard the testimony of someone who had to hit bottom before they would come to their senses.

And then there's the elder brother. Many have failed to include him in the lost category, but he is the main one that applied to the self-righteous Pharisees who were complaining that day. How could one who had always worked so hard and never disobeyed a command of his father be lost? But, in this story, he is the only one left on the outside when this story ends. Jesus wanted them to understand that they were not good enough; they could not earn the favor of God. The only way you get a party is to realize you don't deserve one. Jesus had come into the world not because man was good but because He is good. *"They that are whole need not a physician, but they that are sick."* That lesson was too hard for the religious leaders of that day to accept. And there are those in the world today who feel the same way. In my experience, the hardest people to convert are those who think they are good folk and have never done anything that was very wrong. Oh, they've made some mistakes, but nothing serious. So, they don't need salvation.

But notice how this God feels about each one and what He is willing to do.

Jesus wanted these people and the world to know that this God would leave heaven itself, come to this cesspool of sin and search every dark cave and crevice in search of just one who had wandered away. He would not just look for awhile and then stop but He would search until that lost sheep was found. Then the angels in heaven would throw a party such as one could not imagine.

He wants the world to know that He will leave no stone unturned. No floor will be unswept and no rug will not be looked under. God will search for the one who had been neglected by those who could and should have done something but didn't. When that one is found, heaven will throw another party like the first one.

He wants the world to know that He will sit on the porch and watch and wait until He sees that "no good" prodigal coming. And in spite of the fact he is filthy dirty from the pigpen, his clothes are ragged, he is unshaven and barefoot, and stinks to high heaven; He will run and meet him. He will kiss him; put the best robe on him. Place a ring on his finger, put shoes on his feet, and He will kill the fatted calf. He will throw a party that could be heard from a distance. You ask why? Because *"My son was lost and is found, was dead and is alive again."*

And lastly, He wants the world to know that those who have been and are trying to be good upstanding people, that's well and good. He never wants anyone to stop being good. But, goodness won't make up for the mistakes we all have made. We all still need a Savior. Even though you may think you should not be in the same room with other sinners, this God yearns for all to be inside at the party. This God will humble Himself to the point of going outside and beg the proud self-

216

righteous brother who is pouting because he thinks the party is not for him.

To admit that all are lost, and not just a few of the worst murderers and thieves, is still difficult for some folk. No one is in a position to save themselves. Jesus told a parable of two debtors, one owed a little and the other owed a lot, but He said *"Neither one had anything with which to pay, so he forgave them both."* With nothing to pay, a person is bankrupt; the amount owed makes no difference.

If there is ever a time when a sinner feels like God must not care about him. He should go back and read this chapter and take courage. This is the God who loves sinners and came to seek and save us all. We can be glad this God seeks the lost.

I love the words of the song:

> *"Sinners Jesus will receive: sound the word of grace to all, who the heavenly pathway leave, All who linger all who fall.*
> *Christ receiveth sinful men, even me with all my sin; purged from every spot and stain, Heaven with Him I enter in.*

217

Sing it o'er and o'er again; Christ receiveth sinful men; Make the message clear and plain; Christ receiveth sinful men."
(words by Emma F. Bevan)

And, **THAT'S GOOD NEWS!**